THREE MILITARY LEADERS

THREE MILITARY LEADERS

Heihachiro Togo
•
Isoroku Yamamoto
•
Tomoyuki Yamashita

EDWIN P. HOYT

KODANSHA INTERNATIONAL
Tokyo • New York • London

Distributed in the United States by Kodansha America, Inc., 114 Fifth Avenue, New York New York 10011, and in the United Kingdom and continental Europe by Kodansha Europe, Ltd., 95 Aldwych, London WC2B 4JF.
Published by Kodansha International, Ltd., 17–14 Otowa 1–chome, Bunkyo-ku, Tokyo 112, and Kodansha America, Inc.

First Edition 1993
93 94 95 10 9 8 7 6 5 4 3 2 1

ISBN 4-7700-1737-5

Library of Congress Cataloging-in-Publication Data

Hoyt, Edwin Palmer
   Three Military Leaders: Heihachiro Togo, Isoroku Yamamoto, Tomoyuki Yamashita/by Edwin P. Hoyt.
   p.   cm.
   Includes bibliographical references and index.
   ISBN 4-7700-1737-5
   1. Japan—History—1868—Biography. 2. Japan—History.
   3. Togo, Heihachiro, 1848–1934. 4. Yamamoto, Isoroku, 1884–1943. 5. Yamashita, Tomoyuki, 1885-1846. 6. Japan —History, Military—1868–1945.
I. Titles.
DS881.91.H69 1993
940.54'092'052—dc20
93-24515
  [B]

CONTENTS

Introduction

The Transformation of Japan's Military Tradition

Commodore Matthew Perry's "black ships" forced the opening of Japan to foreign trade in the 1850s, and after that the leaders of Japan struggled for fifteen years with the problems of modernization. At first the forces rallying around the Emperor in Kyoto insisted that the foreigners be ejected, but ultimately they recognized that this was not possible. The growing weakness of the shogunate was becoming apparent and gradually several of the feudal clans changed their allegiance to Kyoto. Between 1862 and 1866 sixty-eight envoys were sent to the west by the *bakufu* (shogunal government) to bring back information about Western life and practices. Representatives of the various clans were also sent, although this was officially forbidden. So about 150 Japanese had studied Western ways intensively before the restoration of the monarchy in 1868.

After the Perry Mission left Japan the shogunate showed interest in acquiring a navy and began to build one with the purchase in Europe of several ships, the most important of which was the full-rigged, three-masted ship *Fuji Yama*. The shogun also brought a British naval mission to Japan to teach the samurai seamanship, and a shipyard was built at Yokosuka, not far from Edo (the modern Tokyo). The

British style of naval uniform was adopted by 1866. Japanese officers were also sent to Holland and other European countries to learn naval skills. In 1866 a Japanese delegation visited America to inquire into the purchase of some ironclad vessels put up for sale following the end of the American Civil War. They bought the *Stonewall Jackson*, which was brought to Japan and renamed the *Azuma*. After the victory of the imperial forces in 1869, resulting in what has become known as the Meiji Restoration, all provincial navies were abolished and their officers and men enrolled in the Imperial Navy. The shogunate had depended on the Dutch for naval advice, but the new Meiji government chose Britain as its model. By 1875 the decision had been made to build a navy capable of carrying on war with other nations and several new ships were ordered from foreign yards.

Besides the navy, a force of some nine thousand troops had been formed to support the new central government by arrangement with the former feudal clans. This force became the nucleus of the modern Japanese Imperial Army.

In spite of the shogunate's intransigence over the matter of foreign influence in the past few centuries, the educated men of Japan had gained a real appreciation of Western cultural and industrial developments, and following the restoration they quickly agreed that emulation was the course to follow. First the feudal system must be abolished—an issue that had to be faced with great care, since so many personal and financial interests were involved. In 1869 the *daimyo* (feudal lords) of Satsuma, Choshu, Tosa, and Hizen presented a joint memorandum to the throne, asking for a complete change in administration. The coordination of this memorandum prevented reform from slipping into factional hands. By the end of that year only seventeen of the nation's feudal lords had not agreed to give up their rights. The *daimyo* became governors. Two years later, on August 29, 1871, feudalism was ended by imperial decree and prefectures took the place of feudal domains. The samurai class was abolished, and the former samurai were forbidden to wear their swords, a practice which had been compulsory under the shogunate. Steps were thus taken to reduce the military nature of the society.

With social liberalization, journalists and others began to press for reforms, including a call for a national army.

The central government grew stronger but continued to experience difficulties in dealing with foreigners, due in part to treaties that had been signed by the shogun's government, beginning in 1858. The treaties gave foreigners the privilege of extraterritoriality, exempting them from responsibility under Japanese law. By 1870 these provisions had become intolerable to many Japanese, and missions were sent abroad to negotiate changes in the so-called "unequal treaties" situation. These missions were also charged with the announced purpose of learning more of foreign ways, and so envoys fanned out to Germany, France, England, the United States, and other nations. They did not make much headway in changing the treaties; the Americans in particular resisted. But the missions did engender goodwill abroad and came home having learned better how to deal with the outside world.

Since the Japanese had been involved mainly with the Dutch, the official language of communication with foreigners had changed from Portuguese to Dutch, but it was not long before the Japanese realized that the major powers they had to deal with were Britain and the United States, and they began to study English.

In 1869 Aritomo Yamagata and Tsugumichi Saigo were sent to Europe for a year to study military methods in France and Germany. On their return they became officials of the Ministry of Military Affairs and applied what they had learned, drafting plans for a conscript army. Tsugumichi Saigo believed in the viability of a conscript army and devised a plan under which men at the age of twenty would be subject to conscription for three years and then serve in the reserve for four years. But his brother, Takamori Saigo, opposed the dissolution of the samurai class, and believed instead that the samurai should become the nucleus of the new army.

Takamori Saigo and several other dissenting ministers left the government and retired to their home provinces. In the first weeks of 1874 the first open ruptures came. Shimpei Ito, one of the disaffected, retired to Saga in Northern Kyushu, and began raiding government offices. This effort was put down and Ito was executed, but other difficulties continued, particularly in Satsuma, in southern Kyushu, where the samurai tradition was very strong, and continued long after the official prohibitions began.

The Meiji government arranged for French officers to take over the training of the new army. By 1875 Japan had a military training school, an arsenal employing 2500 workers, a gunpowder factory and ordnance yard, and a range for artillery training. The role of the military included support of the police in keeping order within Japan, and soldiers were used to put down various peasant revolts and samurai uprisings.

After Takamori Saigo left Tokyo he established a school in Kagoshima—really a military college. It was obvious that trouble lay ahead, and when the further prohibition of the wearing of swords by the general public was announced in 1877, trouble boiled over. Early that year rumors of a plot to murder Saigo created tension, and the government decided to move the arsenal in Kagoshima to a safer place. But the officer sent to supervise this change was not allowed to land. A few days later Saigo led the troops he had been organizing to besiege Kumamoto castle. The time it took him to capture Kumamoto let the imperial forces concentrate their power, and Saigo was forced back to Kagoshima, in turn besieged, and driven from a hill fort by shellfire. Struck in the thigh by a bullet that inflicted a serious wound, he asked a friend to cut off his head so he would not be captured by the imperial forces. The friend obliged and Saigo died, in the fashion of the samurai.

What became known as the Satsuma Rebellion marked the final struggle of the feudal samurai against the government. In 1878 the Army General Staff was established, and a few years later an army staff college was established. The triumph of the conscript army in the Satsuma Rebellion had persuaded even the traditionalists, who had thought that fighting spirit belonged only to the military class.

The later changes were supervised by Taro Katsura and Soroku Kawakami, who had spent several years in Germany studying the military system, and so while the army's original organization was French, the staff system was set up on the German model.

The national government emerged from the rebellion stronger and more resilient than before. The government adopted a progressive policy. No stigma was attached to those who had fought against it, and a temple to the memory of the fallen was erected by public subscription to which members of both sides contributed. A statue of Takamori Saigo was even erected in Tokyo's Ueno Park, where it stands today. Soon the national military was in the hands of the former Satsuma and Choshu clans, where it remained for many years.

The Meiji government began to cast its eyes around Asia with a definite interest in acquiring colonies, to follow the European lead. The Army was enlarged by lengthening the period in the reserves from four years to nine years. The revision soon created an army of 200,000. After 1894 the army was equipped with modern rifles and artillery which soon were all of Japanese manufacture.

The navy received less attention because a navy was an

expensive institution to maintain and at the moment there was no need. The first naval officers training school was established in 1888, although the Navy General Staff was created in 1891. The fleet was small, with only twenty-eight modern ships in service in 1894, displacing an aggregate tonnage of 57,000 tons, plus twenty-four torpedo boats. But the naval planners did well, and although the fleet was small, it had all the facilities needed to maintain and expand it.

After much agitation within Japan and constant pressure for more than a dozen years, in 1894 Great Britain agreed to revision of the "unequal treaties" because their continued effect was to inhibit trade and friendly relations with the Japanese. This change signaled similar agreements with other nations, who did not wish to be slighted by Japan in the process of her modernization and gave in on the question of extraterritoriality with remarkably little trouble.

The constitution was promulgated in 1890 and political parties arose, but under the peculiar nature of the constitution control of the army and the navy were retained in Choshu and Satsuma hands while the political leaders retained control of the Diet. Thus arose a prolonged struggle between the Parliament and the ministers of the government, with the ministers more and more resorting to intervention by the imperial throne to solve problems with the Diet. For example it was not unusual for a government to resign over a question of the budget, and often the military forced the resignation of the government when they objected to economies wrenched out of their budgets.

The Meiji government spent a good deal of money on the military. By 1890 the peacetime military and naval budgets accounted for a third of the national budget. And the services, particularly the army, had a special relationship with the throne. The emperor was commander-in-chief, and he attended parades and maneuvers. Members of the imperial family regularly took up military careers. The chiefs of the army and navy had direct access to the emperor on all military matters. This system was set up to prevent the interference of politicians in the maintenance of safety of the nation. As it turned out, this enabled the military to meddle in politics, and ultimately proved the undoing of the constitutional system, despite the Imperial Rescript to sailors and soldiers in 1885, which called on them to refrain from meddling in politics and to fulfill their duty of loyalty to the country and the throne.

By 1875 the military forces had begun to stir abroad. In that year Japanese survey teams in Korea were attacked by Korean shore batteries and some military action followed. This led to a treaty in 1876 opening Korean ports to Japanese trade. Then began the attempt by Japan to replace China's influence in Korea with her own. In December 1884 Japan tried to stage a coup d'etat in Seoul but failed. By 1894 Japanese influence was such that the government had no hesitation in sending troops into Korea to quell uprisings. The stirrings of imperial ambition had already brought the Japanese takeover of the northern Kuril islands and the Bonin islands and the Ryukyus (which became a Japanese prefecture). Prime Minister Hirobumi Ito and Foreign Minister Munemitsu Mutsu set out to force a confrontation with China over Korea and thus brought on war. By September 1894 the Japanese had control of most of Korea, and the Japanese navy controlled most of the Yellow Sea. Japanese ambitions grew until they went far beyond Korea to include a large cash indemnity and possession of Taiwan and the Liaotung Peninsula. (Eventually they were forced to give back the Liaotung Peninsula in the face of foreign demands and threats of intervention.)

The Japanese began building their own ships as soon as possible. In 1882 they were building wooden ships for their navy and later engines at the Yokosuka dockyard. In 1886 the Japanese launched the *Katsuragi*, the first of their vessels to have twin screws for propulsion. The first truly modern warship acquired was the *Naniwa*, built for Japan in Britain.

By 1887 Japan was building her own steel ships, the first two being the *Akagi* and the *Atago*. In 1895 the *Suma*—the first ship designed and built entirely by the Japanese from keel to topmast—was launched at Yokosuka. From that time on Japan was no longer dependent on foreign shipyards or foreign technicians.

The organization of the Japanese navy was modeled on the British Admiralty, except that the minister of the navy was always an admiral, not a civilian. The original naval force was almost all drawn from the fading samurai class and many of the naval traditions also came from the samurai, as did those of the Japanese army, particularly a refinement of *bushido*, the creed of the samurai. Essentially bushido called for self denial and total loyalty to country and emperor, including a willingness to die for the cause. From the beginning the naval studies included English grammar and conversation. These requirements were listed in the competitive examinations for admission to the Japanese naval academy, along with Chinese literature, Japanese literature, mathematics, and a smattering of sciences.

Although Japan learned army organization from the Europeans, particularly the Germans, the Japanese army from the outset developed its own traditions, chief among them a spartan existence derived from the samurai tradition. Two of its manifestations were the winter and summer marches, in which the army units prided themselves on building character and developing the ability to withstand hardships to a degree not practiced by other armies. In snow marches, held during the coldest months of winter, units went out for three or four days without shelter. The summer marches were held in the hottest weather and after the China war sometimes in the jungles of Southern Taiwan. The men went out to march and bivouack in the open with no head covering other than a service cap. Junior officers suffered the same deprivations as the enlisted men.

No great store was set on appearance; and the spit and polish of other armies was from the first absent in the Japanese army. Officers and men alike seldom shined their boots, and went on parade unshaven (neither was a punishable offense). Japanese army uniforms were baggy and badly fitting, and the generals took pride in the fact that appearance meant nothing, performance everything. The navy set a more rigid standard of neatness but even here simplicity was the norm. Consequently both army and navy tended to be held up to a certain amount of ridicule in Western countries until the Boxer Rebellion and the Russo-Japanese War proved their excellence.

This was the tradition and background of the Imperial Navy and Imperial Army in which Heihachiro Togo, Isoroku Yamamoto, and Tomoyuki Yamashita served. Their experiences, exposure to the Western world, and their reactions to life within the imperial service had a profound effect on the further development of the Japanese military tradition, even in the last days of the twentieth century, long after the transformation of the Imperial Navy and Imperial Army into the three pronged National Self Defense Forces.

PART
I

Heihachiro Togo

Admiral Heihachiro Togo.

1

Heihachiro Togo and Japan's Challenge to the West

Heihachiro Togo was born near Kagoshima in Kyushu in 1848 into a feudal society. No Japanese dared travel abroad nor any foreigner land on Japan's shores lest he risk execution. Two hundred years earlier an imperial edict had declared that "in the future and as long as the sun shall light the world, let no man attempt to land in Japan even as an ambassador and let this order never be infringed on pain of death."

This edict was the result of Japan's first experiences with the West, which had begun in 1542 when a Portuguese ship had stopped in Japan. Soon Christian missionaries followed. They were welcomed by the warlord Nobunaga Oda, as a counterbalance to powerful Buddhist sects which had too much power to suit him. By 1581 the Jesuits had baptized 150,000 people. But in 1587 the new ruler, Hideyoshi, became concerned about the power of the priests. He ordered the Jesuits to leave the country but then changed his mind. Still the seed had been planted. The Japanese *bakufu* learned that the Europeans first Christianized and then colonized. The Jesuits were joined by the Franciscans and Dominicans and they began competing for converts. The shogun Ieyasu Tokugawa, who followed Hideyoshi, began to gain an unfavorable impression of the Christians, aided by the Dutch and an English advisor named Will Adams. Ieyasu finally decided to prohibit the Christian religion in Japan. In 1616 the new shogun, Hidetada, declared war on Christianity and set about exterminating Japanese Christians. Soon the European influence was hanging on by a slender thread, and then it was nothing but a fading memory. All the missionaries were gone, and most of their converts were dead. In 1635 alone, about 280,000 Japanese Christians were put to death. The anti-Christian drive continued. The Dutch helped with the guns of their warships to subdue the last stronghold, the fortress of Amakusa, in 1638. After that the Dutch were almost alone among the foreigners who remained, trading through a single facility on the island of Dejima in Nagasaki Harbor.

But by the middle of the nineteenth century Japan's isolation was coming to an end. Five years after Togo's birth, Commodore Matthew Perry appeared in Tokyo Bay with his black ships and the demand that Japan be opened to foreign trade.

By 1855 Japan had been opened to foreigners, and European nations were hoping to colonize the country. Despite internal quarrels, all Japan was united in feeling that foreigners must not be allowed to take control. The shogun's advisors recognized the need to modernize or be conquered. And as a result a national navy was formed in 1855, when the shogunate ordered a warship from the Dutch, and the Dutch navy sent officers to teach the samurai how to operate it.

Togo's father, Kichizaemon, was a samurai who had held many important offices in the service of the Satsuma daimyo. The boy received a samurai education, first at home, then at a local school and then at the College of Kagoshima, where he studied Chinese classical literature, calligraphy, history and Japanese literature. As a youth Heihachiro showed no unusual qualities, except diligence.

When he became 13, society considered him to be an adult, and he was appointed as a copyist in the Satsuma administration. But—it was a mark of the times—he also spent many hours drilling and studying the martial arts in the new military fashion, and also learning how to use artillery.

In 1862 the peace that had accompanied the foreigners' coming to Japan was rudely interrupted by several incidents. As far as Togo was concerned, the most important one was the killing in Satsuma of a British merchant named Charles Lenox Richardson, for not showing enough respect to a column of samurai on the road. The British government took exception to the killing and demanded indemnification and the punishment of the murderers. The daimyo of Satsuma, who did not regard the killing as murder, refused to pay, although the shogun's government ordered him to do so. As a result the British sent warships to Kagoshima. The daimyo

A samurai rifle squadron of the Satsuma domain, during the latter years of the shogunate preceding the Meiji Restoration.

called his samurai to defend the city, including Kichizaemon Togo and his three sons, Shirobei, Sokoro, and Heihachiro. The samurai, who functioned as both army and navy, wore their usual costume of armor, two swords, and a round helmet bearing their family crests.

The defense of Kagoshima in August 1863 offers a good comparison of Japanese military capabilities of the time with those of the Westerners. The city had ten forts, 105 old-fashioned muzzle-loading cannon, three steamships and twelve thirty-five-foot junks. The British came in with a squadron equipped with modern rifled guns and anchored in Kagoshima Bay. The commander demanded indemnification and the trial and punishment of the murderers of Merchant Richardson. Since the daimyo was absent in Kirishima, three days' journey away, affairs were handled by his advisors. The British gave them twenty-four hours to answer the demands.

The daimyo's samurai were called to drive the invaders away. The defense plan consisted of a scheme to overwhelm the enemy, kill the officers of the flagship HMS *Euryalus* and disperse the British fleet. The Satsuma commander announced that he had an answer to the British demands, and asked leave to board the *Euryalus* to deliver it, along with his escort. But the suspicious British authorized the general to come aboard accompanied by only two officers. The response was a request for a conference. The British refused, the Satsuma general was rowed ashore with all honors, and the samurai assembled in the forts, while the people of Kagoshima gathered in the temples to pray for another Divine Wind to destroy the British as the famous *Kamikaze* had dispersed the forces of Kublai Khan five centuries before.

A storm did blow up that day. The harbor became rough and dangerous and the British men-of-war shifted anchorage to the lee of the volcanic island of Sakurajima. That evening the sky grew dark and the seas were flecked with white foam. By dawn the storm was in full force. The British ships moved again, but not in retreat. They sailed right into the heart of the harbor where the three Satsuma steamers were moored and captured them. That morning orders were given by the samurai general to open fire on the British enemy, and the forts prepared for action.

Heihachiro Togo was one of the gunners. They heated their cannon balls in furnaces behind the batteries, rammed powder down the muzzles of the guns, and then dirt, to prevent the red-hot cannon balls from touching the powder and going off prematurely. Then the cannon balls were rammed in, and the detonating powder was placed in the breech. The aimers aimed, the gunners ignited the detonators, and the guns began to fire. They did not do much damage. The British did not immediately respond because Admiral Kuper, the British commander, first burned the steamers. Then the fleet turned its attention to the forts on the shore. The ships fired in broadsides, sailing and steaming in a parallel line with the coast. They engaged one fort after another, then turned about and returned to fire once more.

A contemporary Japanese depiction of the bombardment of Kagoshima by British naval forces in 1863.

The samurai fired as long as they could. By noon they were running out of ammunition. The general ordered his men to the beach, where they stood, brandishing their swords and halberds, challenging the British to come and fight like Japanese warriors.

But the British paid no attention. They sailed back and forth across the bay, bombarding the ten forts with their rifled guns until they had accomplished enormous destruction. When night fell, the British anchored again in the lee of Sakurajima. That night, as the British ships' bands played, the high winds of the storm spread the fires ignited by the bombardment into the city, and Kagoshima burned.

Next morning, after a few parting shots, the British fleet moved out. The battle had cost the British thirteen sailors dead and sixty-three wounded. They had burned the forts and the town. The Japanese casualties were never counted. The British were satisfied that they had exacted proper punishment. But the samurai were greeted as heroes in Satsuma. The British had not landed, and so, by traditional Japanese standards, the warriors had won a victory. But when the daimyo came back from Kirishima, he took another view. His forts were gone. His modern warships were gone. Was that victory? No, Satsuma would have to learn how to fight the Westerners using modern methods. And so Kichizaemon Togo advised his three sons to enroll in the new Satsuma naval force, and eventually all three of them took his advice. Heihachiro Togo was on his way to help build a modern Japanese navy. He was eighteen years old and the year was 1866.

2

Cadet Togo Learns the Naval Trade

In the year 1866, when the young samurai Heihachiro Togo elected to join the Satsuma daimyo's navy, Shogun Iyemochi died. His successor, Yoshinobu, had no taste for power. By November that year Yoshinobu gave up power, and the strength of the government was in the hands of the *dajokan*, an executive body dominated by the Satsuma and Choshu clans, whose principal object at the moment was the eradication of the shogunate. Thus began a war that lasted for more than a year. Heihachiro Togo participated in this war as a naval gunner.

A few years earlier the shogun had sent Admiral Enomoto to Holland to learn the arts of Western naval warfare, and he returned honor bound to fight for his leader. He challenged the Satsuma navy, which was headed by Genroku Atatsuka. During the first part of the war, the Satsuma navy did most of its fighting ashore and it consisted of raids and surprise attacks. One of Admiral Enomoto's ships was an American paddle-wheel steamer that had been built for use in the American Civil War. It ravaged the Satsuma coast and on one occasion steamed into a Satsuma port flying U.S. colors, and then headed for an enemy ship. The crew grappled and boarded and captured her. This ruse was regarded as completely acceptable by the samurai who fought the war. One of the adages of the *bushido* code was "Win first, and fight later." Victory in battle meant everything, no matter how it was attained.

But one day the daimyo bought a 1200-ton paddle steamer that had been built at Cowes, England. She had been named the *Kiang-tse*, but the daimyo rechristened her the *Kasuga*. Samurai Togo went aboard as a junior officer and gunner. The *Kasuga* steamed around the Inland Sea, and ultimately came into contact with Admiral Enomoto's flagship, the screw steamer *Kaiyo*. In the battle that followed, called the Battle of the Awa Coast, gunner Togo fired a shot that carried away one of the *Kaiyo*'s masts. Admiral Enomoto's fleet was soon wiped out, and when he surrendered the naval war was over. Togo was promoted to the rank of officer of the third class.

After the war the Satsuma navy was dissolved and Togo joined the Imperial Navy. He had to begin at the bottom as an apprentice officer. His first assignment was to learn English, for the organizers of the navy wanted to send a number of young men to England for training. He began study under a Japanese official who knew the language and then moved to a government school. On January 31, 1871, he became a midshipman in the Imperial Navy. He was assigned to the training ship *Ryogo*. A few months later he was selected as one of a group of twelve Japanese midshipmen sent to England to train under the Royal Navy. They boarded an English ship at Yokohama, and sailed for Hong Kong, and then through the Indian Ocean. They disembarked at Suez and traveled on to Alexandria by camel, and then boarded ship again in the Mediterranean, bound for England. At the end of May, 1871, they passed Gibraltar, then moved up the Atlantic coast of Spain and France and into the English Channel.

The ship was met at Southampton by members of the

Japanese embassy staff, and the dozen young men were whisked off to a London tailor for Western-style uniforms.

At first the young Japanese were lodged at a hotel and shown the sights of London, from the trooping of the guard at St. James's Palace, to the waterfront docks. They even went to the theater. But in a few days the sightseeing ended and it was down to the business of learning how to become navy sailors. The young men were separated, sent to boarding houses and told to perfect their English. Togo went to Plymouth. There he began to learn something about the Royal Navy. He wandered around Plymouth that summer talking to people to better his English and spending a good deal of time at the docks looking at ships.

The Japanese government had wanted its young men to take the regular naval training of British officers, but the British were not willing to undertake this. In the fall of 1871 Togo was enrolled in a naval preparatory school under a clergyman headmaster to study history, mathematics, and engineering draftsmanship. From there in 1872 he went to the Thames Nautical Training College. Training was aboard a three-masted sailing ship, HMS *Worcester*, which was moored in the Thames river.

Cadet Togo soon realized that his former training as a samurai sailor and a junior officer in the Japanese Imperial Navy was of little use. Western methods were entirely different from anything he had learned. And he had to learn how to reason like an Englishman if he was to solve the problems set before him. This task was formidable, but he persevered and did learn.

His British companions called him Johnny Chinaman, a name he did not like and which led to blows more than once. The name stuck, although his willingess to fight English-style brought him a new respect. The British were so insensitive to other people that they could not understand why he objected to being called Chinese. To the British all yellow men were Chinese, and Togo was a yellow man, therefore why in the world would he object?

But by the end of the two-year training period Togo's British classmates had learned a thing or two. To everyone's astonishment, Cadet Togo passed second in his class.

After two years aboard the ship *Worcester*, the cadets were taken to sea aboard the training ship *Hampshire*. They sailed out of the Thames at the end of February, 1875, and headed for deep water. On April 19 they rounded the Cape of Good Hope and seventy days later they reached Melbourne. During their time there Cadet Togo visited several Pacific islands. On July 11 the *Hampshire* set sail from Melbourne on her return voyage around Cape Horn, at the tip of South America, and at the end of September she returned to the Thames. The voyage had covered thirty thousand miles, around the world.

Imagine all the new sights Heihachiro Togo had witnessed and all the insights he had gained in these four years! A boy from Japan, having been sequestered all his life and knowing nothing about the outside world, suddenly thrust into the heart of Western civilization and then into the Pacific. The shock had been enormous but in those years Togo had learned how Westerners behaved, and more important, how they thought.

His next task was to master higher mathematics. This program had all been arranged by the Japanese embassy. He was sent to Cambridge to study with the Rev. A.D. Capel. He settled down to a life of study, and made more efforts to learn English ways, now that he knew the language fairly well. He was exposed to Christianity when he went to Methodist church services with the Capel family.

In Cambridge, Togo developed a disease of the eye which threatened his sight. For weeks he said nothing about it, fearing that he would have to give up his naval career, but eventually the pain became so severe that he had to confide in the Rev. Mr. Capel. The minister forthwith reported to the Japanese embassy, Togo was whisked up to London, and Harley Street ophthalmologists saved his vision.

Meanwhile, in Tokyo, changes had come to the Imperial Navy. The original plan had been for the twelve cadets to remain three years and then come home to Japan to begin practicing their newfound skills. But in the interim, the new naval ministry had become conscious of its need to create a modern seagoing navy and had ordered the building of three warships to the most modern British standards. The young naval officers would remain in England, where they would inspect the progress of the shipbuilding. When the vessels were completed they would sail home in them. Togo was ordered to oversee the building of the *Fuso*, which was under construction in London in a shipyard at Poplar. He returned to take lodgings in Greenwich and thereafter every day Togo went to Poplar, to watch the progress of his ship. At night he wrote up his notes.

Then came an event in Japan that shook Heihachiro Togo as profoundly as had the difficulty with his eyesight. The men around the Emperor Meiji had not been idle in the years since Togo had been sent abroad. They were briskly reorganizing Japanese society and changing its structure, destroying the ancient warrior class. This effort was masked by new laws that forbade criticism of the government's policies, but underneath rebellion was brewing and one of the major leaders of the samurai was Takamori Saigo, who had once been an ardent supporter of the Meiji monarchy, but who had soured on politics and retired to run a school for young samurai in Kagoshima. The new government restrictions weighed heavily on the rebels, as they saw their livelihood cut off. Their only alternative to civilian life was to lay down the two swords of the samurai and join the new military, which meant a sacrifice of status. Saigo was trying another alternative, to convert the samurai from warriors into bureaucrats. Why not? They were the best educated men in Japan. All they required was to learn the ways of the modern world, and these could be taught to them while they kept their privileged status.

But it was not to be. In 1876 the ardent men of the oligarchy that ran the country grew impatient and disestablished the samurai altogether. This was a severe blow to Saigo, wrecking all his plans to save the samurai class. He began to resist the change. The new administration in Tokyo got wind of it, and in 1877 issued orders that the important arsenals in Satsuma be closed down and the weapons transferred to other areas of whose loyalty to the throne the rulers were more certain. This was the final insult as far as Saigo

This statue of Takamori Saigo was erected in Tokyo's Ueno Park a few years after his death in an abortive insurrection against the national government.

was concerned and he rebelled, seized the arsenals, and led a force of 15,000 men in open rebellion against the Meiji authorities.

Togo's shock at learning of the Satsuma Rebellion was intensified when he discovered that his mother, his brothers and other relatives were all deeply involved in it. He met with others of the young officers in London who shared the difficulty. What were they to do? Several of the officers wanted to leave for Japan immediately. Togo counseled against it. Then should they not send apologies to the Imperial Throne for the behavior of their relatives? Togo counseled against that, also. For himself, he said, he felt no responsibility for what his brothers and other members of his family did. They were citizens of Satsuma, with loyalties that went back for generations. It was understandable that they would follow the Satsuma lead. But for himself, he was of the new generation of Japanese, and his loyalty was to the throne and the government that had sent him to England. He would stay and finish his job showing that he was grateful for all the advantages offered to him. His views did not change although his brothers engaged in bloody battle with the government he served. His elder brother, Sokuro, was killed in the last great battle at Shiroyama, when Saigo and his army were destroyed by the government forces, but this did not alter Togo's views. His destiny was inextricably linked with modern Japan. He belonged to the present and the future, not the past.

3

Japan's New Navy

In February 1878, the warship *Fuso* was completed, fitted out and ready to go to Japan. Sublieutenant Heihachiro Togo sailed in her. When they reached Yokohama the *Fuso* and the two ships that accompanied her were greeted royally by an enormous crowd of well-wishers. The young officers had been abroad for seven years; their country was enormously changed and new tall buildings were going up in Yokohama and Tokyo.

The Imperial Navy had a good idea of what it wanted. The navy had established a naval college at Tsukiji, where thirty British officers taught young Japanese. The returnees gave some lectures there, and then they were posted from one ship to another. Sublieutenant Togo went from the *Fuso* to the *Hiei* and back again.

His seven years of service at lowly rank were not forgotten in Tokyo. Eighteen months after his return home he was promoted to lieutenant commander in the modernized Japanese Navy and assigned as first lieutenant (executive officer) of the royal yacht *Jingei*. Here he distinguished himself by his attention to duty. He knew more about seamanship than any man aboard the vessel, and also knew how to approach problems directly, a skill he had mastered in the British service. When a fellow officer protested that Lieutenant Commander Togo was not issuing orders in the proper offical way of the Imperial Navy, Togo said that what was important was that the orders be clearly understood.

As first lieutenant, Lieutenant Commander Togo stood next in line to the captain, bearing responsibility for the *Jingei*'s wellbeing, including discipline, performance, and morale throughout the ship. He did the job thoroughly. He never seemed to sleep, in the opinion of one officer. Every time the officer came on deck—morning, noon, or night—he found Lieutenant Commander Togo there. No one regarded him as a brilliant officer, but nothing went wrong aboard the *Jingei* when he was first lieutenant. His attributes were attention to detail, steadiness of performance, and imperturbability. No matter what happened he did not get excited nor make mistakes.

While Lieutenant Commander Togo served on the *Jingei*, he got married. The marriage was arranged by a *baikainin* or go-between. Togo was familiar with the family of the girl, Tetsuko. She was the daughter of a noble samurai of Satsuma, and the marriage was a good one for him. But he had never seen her before their first arranged meeting.

Shortly after the wedding in 1881, Togo went back to sea, while Tetsuko lived with his mother for a year. The couple later bought a house in Tokyo, where they were to live for the rest of their lives.

After two years on the *Jingei* Lieutenant Commander Togo was ordered to the *Amagi*, a wooden ship of only 600 tons, and one of the oldest vessels in the Japanese Navy. It looked like a demotion, but Togo did not complain. Instead he turned the old tub into a spit-and-polish naval vessel.

In July 1882 the *Amagi* was calling at the port of Shimonoseki, near the Korea Strait, when the captain received a war alert. The Japanese Embassy in Seoul had been attacked by Korean soldiers and civilians. A number of staff members had been killed, and Minister Hanabusa and a few of his people had managed to escape to Chemulpo (Inchon), and then to board a junk which had foundered near a small island off the coast. They had been picked up by a British warship and brought to Nagasaki.

The Japanese government suspected that China was responsible for the incident. For centuries Korea had been a Chinese vassal state, but in recent years the Japanese had turned their eyes toward Seoul. In 1876 Japan had forced a trade treaty on the Koreans. It had been greeted with riots and anti-Japanese demonstrations. China had not failed to notice the Japanese interest, and the dowager empress's government had been intriguing ever since. The Japanese claimed that the gold of Li Hung-chang, the empress's chief minister, had paid for the attack on the Japanese embassy.

The Imperial Navy was ready for war, and Togo and the others were hoping it would come. The government at Tokyo considered the matter for three days and on the fourth day ordered the ships at Shimonoseki to sail for Korea and reinstall the Japanese minister, by force if necessary. Admiral Nire was given the expedition. Eight ships were to do the job. One of them was the *Amagi*.

So the *Amagi* and the seven other Japanese warships sailed to Korea. They faced great difficulties. They had no charts of Korean waters and knew nothing about the tides (Chemulpo's tide is the most extreme in Asia). They waited for a ship to come out of the harbor and then followed her wake in. As they moved into the Chemulpo harbor they met Chinese warships under Admiral Ting Ju-chang, who informed the Japanese that the Chinese were also in Korea to restore order.

The Japanese landed a force to march on Seoul. Lieutenant Commander Togo was in command of the *Amagi* contingent. The force reached Seoul without opposition, and returned the Japanese minister to his ministry. When the

Koreans balked at paying Japan reparations for the attack on their ministry, the Japanese ships prepared to open fire. The Koreans then backed down, and further incident was prevented.

Japan had already embarked on its course of empire, although at first it did not have the military strength to move very fast. As its strength grew, so did Japanese ambitions. The naval task force was left at Chemulpo for six months "to strengthen Korean independence." The fleet charted Korean waters for the future and on this duty the *Amagi* made a trip up the Taedong river.

In the winter of 1883 the Korean adventure came to an end and the *Amagi* returned to Japan. There, at the naval station of Bakan, Togo was involved in an incident that revealed to the Imperial Navy a hitherto hidden aspect of his character—blind stubbornness. This trait had first become apparent to his family when he was a boy. He had played a trick on his elder brother, dosing a glass of water with red pepper. When his father insisted that Togo apologize to his brother, Togo refused, and was punished by banishment from the family. He never did apologize, but was finally reinstated without doing so. Now the same stubbornness combined with xenophobia manifested itself in an incident involving a British warship that had entered the Japanese harbor. As was the custom, it was saluted by the *Amagi* firing its guns. The British captain said not enough guns had been fired to give the warship her due. So Togo fired more guns. Still not enough, said the British captain. He asked that the salute be repeated. Togo refused. If the captain would add the two sets of salutes, he would see that it was enough, said Lieutenant Commander Togo. This was a unique interpretation of naval courtesy. The British protested to the Navy Ministry at Tokyo but nothing further was said of the incident.

Lieutenant Commander Togo was shortly afterward

given command of his own ship, the *Daini Tihu*. She was a very small vessel, 135 feet long and displacing 125 tons. Her duty was to guard the Inland Sea coast from Kure to Sasebo. This dull but necessary service occupied Togo until May of 1884, when he was given command of the *Amagi* and ordered to Shanghai to join the Middle Fleet commanded by Admiral Matsumura. Japan was joining the British, American and Germans to send naval forces into China "to protect the lives and property of their citizens." The immediate reason was a crisis between China and France. But what it meant to Japan was that twenty years after foreigners had tried to take control of Japan, Japan had risen so far in world esteem that she was now numbered among the powers, although her strength at the moment was minimal. Secretly the Japanese were ordered to use this opportunity to observe the operational methods of the British, Americans and Germans.

So Captain Togo went to Shanghai in his little vessel and then had orders to steam up the Yangtze River. He steamed as far as Hankow, which at that time was the furthest upriver a foreign vessel had gone, six hundred miles into the interior of China.

During his months in China, Captain Togo spoke little but observed much. He noted that the Chinese equipment was outmoded, and worse than that, it was not properly maintained. This condition meant serious failures in the organization of the Chinese Navy, and a major weakness.

The troubles between the French and the Chinese developed into a minor war—really a French punitive expedition against China to further French ambitions in Indo-China. Where the French fleet went, whether to Hong Kong or Taiwan, Captain Togo's ship followed, and Togo reported to Tokyo on the French and their activities. His tour lasted until the end of October, when his ship returned to Shanghai and Togo made a long report to Admiral Matsumura. The report was well received in Tokyo, and at the end of the year, Togo was recalled to Japan and invited to a banquet given by the emperor.

Already the Japanese had recognized their needs if they were to compete with the Western powers. While China bought her arms abroad, the Japanese decided to take the longer but more independent course of producing their own. By 1885 the keels of three warships had been laid at Onahama and the engines were built at the Yokosuka docks. Under foreign teachers, Japanese learned to be naval architects, draftsmen, and skilled craftsmen. Togo was at the heart of this, because he was one of the few Japanese who knew something about foreign shipbuilding, having watched the construction of the *Fuso* in the British shipyard. He was promoted to commander in June 1885 and sent to Onahama shipyard to supervise the building of the *Yamato*. When she was built, he was given command and promoted to captain. He was not quite thirty-nine years old.

But then, just when Togo's career seemed to have blossomed, he was stricken with rheumatic arthritis. He could no longer function on the bridge of the *Yamato* and had to be relieved of command. He spent the next year virtually bedridden, and by the fall of 1887 was still ill. He was kept on sick leave by the admiralty. He spent his time reading works on international law and diplomacy, and finally two full years after his illness began he started to regain his health and strength. It is a measure of his recognized value to the admiralty that he had not been forcibly retired during those two years. But he was recovering and by mid-May 1890 he was back on active duty as chief of staff to the commander of the naval base at Kure.

While he he was serving there, Chinese Admiral Ting appeared with his fleet on a "good-will" mission. Actually, the purpose was to show off the two new warships the Chinese had acquired from German yards, the *Ting Yuen* and the *Chen Yuen*. They were armored cruisers, displacing 7500 tons, and each carried four twelve-inch guns in double turrets. When the *Ting Yuen* required some repair work it was done at Kure. The Chinese paid no attention to a common-looking middle-aged man in plain clothes who was poking around the yard when the ship was in dock. The man was Captain Togo, and he was paying close attention to the vessel. Later, when fellow officers commented that the Chinese warships would be formidable fighters with their twelve-inch guns, he disagreed. The Chinese were not maintaining their equipment properly, and any twelve-inch guns that were used primarily as clotheslines to dry the crew's laundry were not going to be very effective in battle.

Captain Togo was next sent to supervise the building of underwater defenses in the Strait of Shimonoseki. The Imperial Navy command was now sure he was restored to good health, and he was given command of the new British-built steel ship *Naniwa*, which carried two ten-inch guns and six six-inch guns and could make a speed of eighteen knots. She also was fitted with six torpedo tubes.

After taking command of the *Naniwa*, he carried out a hydrographic survey of the Ryukyu archipelago and of Honshu island. Then in January 1893 Captain Togo received orders to go to Hawaii, where a band of American-born residents had just fomented a revolution against Queen Liliuokalani's monarchy. His assignment was to protect the life and property of the Japanese residents, who numbered about 22,000. Captain Togo proved as obdurate in Hawaii as he had been with the British man of war in Japanese waters. He refused to salute the new government as the American ships and others were doing. An escaping Japanese prisoner swam to the ship; Togo took him aboard and refused to surrender the man to the new authorities. He finally gave him up to the Japanese consul, but only after receiving orders from Tokyo.

The *Naniwa* stayed in Hawaii for two months. When the

revolution turned out to be successful, Togo was ordered back to Japan. Disturbances soon broke out again, and the ship was then sent back to Hawaii again. The Japanese government by 1893 was ready to flex its muscles but there were no incidents involving the Japanese, and that spring the *Naniwa* was relieved by another Japanese warship and went back to Japan. Captain Togo was assigned to take command of the Kure naval base. He would rather have been at sea, but he was getting valuable administrative experience that would prepare him for higher command.

4

The Sino-Japanese War

In July 1894, Captain Togo fired what was to be the first shot of the Sino-Japanese War. Neither China nor Japan had declared war, but it was nevertheless imminent and everyone knew it. Both countries were sending troops to Korea "to maintain order," which meant to maintain influence over Korea. The Chinese government had for the first time declared officially to Japan that Korea was a Chinese vassal state. Since Japanese plans for their empire included Korea, this statement created a crisis in Tokyo. The Japanese foreign office and the army and navy all prepared for war even though the Japanese Ambassador at St. Petersburg warned that if war arose between China and Japan, and particularly over Korea, the Russian government was likely to enter on the side of China. The Russians had an abiding interest in Korea for commercial reasons as well as its warm-water ports, and their relations with China were much better than their relations with Japan. The Czar's government regarded Japan as ambitious and a potential enemy.

Despite that severe warning, the Japanese government decided to proceed to go to war with China. Munemitsu Mutsu, the foreign minister, saw this as a propitious time to create an empire and the army and the naval establishment was itching for a war, and willing to take enormous risks. They had learned well from the West that the way of empire was the way of power. They knew that they had already created a military force far superior to that of the Chinese, and they were burning to extend the empire, to put Japan on a par with the European powers. The leaders favored the policy enunciated by Lord Masayoshi Hatta in the 1850s, when he had suggested that the Japanese pretend to accept the Western economic invasion of Japan, bide their time, and be prepared to take over the domination of Asia at some point when the Western powers were otherwise occupied.

Captain Togo, returned to command of the *Naniwa*, was told to prepare for war. On July 23 the Japanese fleet put to sea. Three armored cruisers, including the *Naniwa*, left the main body of the fleet and steamed for Asan on the west Korean coast, looking for trouble. When the *Naniwa* encountered the Chinese cruiser *Chi Yuen*, Captain Togo had no hesitation in opening fire. His contention about the weakness of the Chinese cruisers was proved to be correct, and soon the *Chi Yuen* was blazing and out of action. She fled. Togo pursued her, but was diverted by encountering the *Kowshing*, a British steamer in the service of the Chinese government, which was carrying a Chinese general and 1100 of his troops to Korea. Togo ordered the British ship to stop, and when she stopped, he engaged in a long conversation by signal flag with the steamer. The end came when the Chinese general arrested the British captain and refused to let the captain or crew leave the ship. Thereupon the *Naniwa* sank her.

The British captain and crew took to the boats, and most were rescued, including a German major who was coming to observe the activities in Korea. The Japanese not only sank the *Kowshing*, but they machine-gunned the Chinese survivors in the water, a fact attested to by the German major, although officially denied by the Japanese government.

Given the training and philosophy of the Japanese from samurai days this was not an unusual action. Generosity to enemies was not a Japanese military attribute then or later.

The sinking of the *Kowshing* caused a furor in Japan. At first the government was upset because a vessel flying the British flag had been sunk. Officials in Tokyo were worried about repercussions. Captain Togo got a very bad press, and the general public was opposed to what he had done. But when nothing untoward came of the incident save a British warning about the sinking of British ships, the attitude was reversed. Press and public began to lionize Captain Togo and he became the first hero of the Sino-Japanese war.

War was declared on August 1. The gamble was successful, for the Russians did not intervene. By that time Captain Togo's act of violence had been followed by an attack on the Chinese at Asan by Japanese General Oshima, and the defeat of the Chinese. Six weeks later the Japanese and Chinese navies fought the first modern naval battle in history, using ironclad and steel vessels with rifled guns. It was called the Battle of the Yellow Sea, or the Battle of the Yalu. It occurred on September 17, 1894, in the bay of Korea, off the island of Haiyang. Admiral Tsuboi, commanding the Japanese fleet, sighted the Chinese fleet and moved to engage.

The Chinese had five ironclad warships, seven unarmored ships, four torpedo boats, and three gunboats. The Japanese had seven modern ironclad cruisers, and five unarmored ships, twelve in all. The Chinese ships were better armored, but the Japanese had the striking power, 70 large guns against 55 large Chinese guns.

Shortly before 1 p.m., when the two fleets were about 6000 yards apart, the Chinese began firing. The Japanese continued to advance, but they did not fire. Then at 4000 yards the Japanese fleet began firing. The Japanese had changed formation and now prepared to cross the Chinese fleet's T, which meant that all the Japanese guns could be trained on the Chinese fleet, while the Chinese could only fire their forward turrets against the Japanese. Soon two of the Chinese warships were afire. One sank and the other fled.

The *Naniwa* got separated from the Japanese squadron and came under heavy Chinese fire. Togo remained on his bridge, apparently impassive. The *Naniwa* came under attack from the Chinese torpedo boats, but machine gun fire drove the Chinese off.

The flagship *Matsushima* later was hit by a Chinese shell that did great damage but the Chinese battleship *Ting Yuen* was set afire. The *Chen Yuen* had also been hit several times. Just before dark, when the fleets were approaching the mouth of the Yalu River, they broke off the engagement. During the night the Chinese put in at Port Arthur (Dalian). The battle was over. The Chinese had lost five ships and the Japanese fleet had suffered serious damage to the *Matsushima* and lesser damage to three other warships. Nine Chinese shells had hit the *Naniwa*, but not a single man was killed or wounded. More than a thousand Chinese sailors had been killed, and 90 Japanese, with 200 wounded. The Chinese claimed a victory, but the facts pointed the other way. Still the battle was not decisive; the two German-built Chinese battleships were still afloat and the naval war would have to be fought again.

On November 21 the Japanese army captured Port Arthur. The Western world, which had anticipated a Chinese victory, was astounded. On December 18 the Japanese bombarded Chefoo, fifty miles west of Weihaiwei, the big Chinese naval base.

Captain Togo's *Naniwa* participated in this bombardment along with the cruisers *Yoshino* and *Akitsushima*. This operation was really a feint, to mask the landing of Japanese troops at Yung-cheng, fifty miles east of Weihaiwei, where the Chinese fleet had taken refuge.

On January 1895, the Japanese Army marched from

Yung-cheng to Weihaiwei and attacked the forts defending the eastern approaches. As the Rising Sun flag went up above the forts, the Chinese ships in the harbor opened fire. On January 30 Captain Togo led a naval bombardment on the forts that guarded the entrance to the Weihaiwei harbor, with the *Naniwa*, *Akitsushima*, and *Katsuragi*. They blew up the port ammunition depot but did not destroy the forts.

As the month of February began, the weather took a turn for the worse, and the bulk of the Japanese fleet sought refuge in the port of Yung-cheng as the army consolidated its hold on the environs of Weihaiwei. But Captain Togo's *Naniwa* and her sister ships of the First Light Flotilla patrolled off Weihaiwei to prevent the escape of the Chinese fleet. In this dangerous weather, Captain Togo spent day and night on his bridge, tortured by the return of his arthritis, but refusing to give in.

On February 3, when the storm began to slack off, Admiral Ito entrusted Captain Togo with the attack on Weihaiwei. It was carried out by torpedo boats, beginning on the afternoon of February 4, when Torpedo Boat No. 6 managed to break through the boom which closed the harbor. The next morning at 4 a.m. Togo sent four torpedo boats in an attack on the western entrance, a diversionary attack to attract the attention of the Chinese fleet. At the same time Admiral Ito sent ten torpedo boats against the east entrance to the harbor. In the fight that followed the *Ting Yuen* was hit and went up on the rocks.

On February 6, the torpedo boats attacked again and sank the *Lai Yuen*. On February 7, Admiral Ito launched a general assault by his fleet. The last twelve Chinese torpedo boats came out to fight, but ten of them were sunk or captured by Captain Togo's light cruisers. The Japanese continued to bombard the harbor, and by February 11 nearly all of Admiral Ting's Chinese ships were sunk. Ashore, only the fort of Huang-tao still fired on the Japanese. On February 11 Admi-

ral Ito launched the final attack. Captain Togo's light cruisers engaged the fort all night. On the morning of February
12 a lone Chinese gunboat came out of the east entrance
heading for the Japanese flagship. The gunboat was carrying
a flag of truce. As Admiral Ting's officers surrendered the
fleet, Admiral Ting took poison aboard his flagship and
died. A few days later when the Japanese sent another expeditionary force to land at Shanhaikwan, only 175 miles from
Peking, the Chinese sent a mission to Japan to sue for peace.

Japan had won the war, but on March 15, 1895, the very
day that the Chinese minister Li Hung-cheng left China for
Tokyo, a Japanese fleet sailed from Sasebo for Taiwan to
seize the island and the Pescadores islands. The fleet was led
by the First Light Flotilla, now under command of Rear
Admiral Heihachiro Togo. When the fleet reached the
islands, he supervised the landings. Admiral Togo had
arrived in the highest naval council of Japan.

That spring, in spite of the treaty giving Japan control of
Taiwan, rebellious Chinese elements continued to fight, and
Togo led the Japanese forces that first besieged and then
captured the island. By October 1895, Togo was in supreme
command of the naval forces in Taiwan waters. He remained
until November 16, when he was recalled to Japan. There he
was feted, awarded the Order of the Golden Falcon and the
Order of the Rising Sun, promoted to the Council of Admirals, and made chairman of the Naval Technical Board.

The world marveled at this unexpected victory of Japan
in the war against China, but soon attributed it to the ineptitude of the Chinese forces. The Japanese were not given the
credit due for creating a first class military machine in just
over twenty years. They were deprived of part of their fruits
of victory, the Liaotung Peninsula of Manchuria, when a
consortium of European nations virtually forced them to surrender the claim in exchange for a cash indemnity. Admiral
Togo was as annoyed and resentful of this Western attitude

as any other officer. But at the moment there was nothing to be done, but again to bide their time.

In 1896 Togo became Chairman of the Advanced Naval College. He progressed steadily, because he was recognized as one of the most learned as well as the most aggressive of the Japanese naval officers. He was promoted to vice admiral. He became commander of the naval base at Sasebo, where he was responsible for many developments in the modernizing of the Japanese fleet. He also spent as much time at sea as possible, and made a special study of the Tsushima Strait, which he recognized as vital in the defenses of Japan. On May 20, 1900, he was made admiral of the fleet. It was apparent that there would soon be work for him at sea, because the Boxer Uprising in China had begun, and the Japanese as well as other foreigners were in danger in Peking.

On June 12, 1900, the counselor of the Japanese legation at Peking was assassinated and his body was mutilated. In Tokyo the Japanese government gave Admiral Togo orders to sail for China and on June 22 he arrived off Taku to join the international fleet that represented eight nations. While waiting there for international agreement on a course of action, he made a study of the warships of the other nations and concluded that the Russian Navy was not nearly so strong as its enthusiasts claimed. He was particularly impressed by the slackness of the discipline and training.

"The Russians are much too ready to use their warships as freighters for military supplies. Any ship used frequently as a cargo carrier loses her fighting quality," Admiral Togo reported to the naval authorities.

It was obvious even then that Admiral Togo considered the Russians to be a potential enemy, and indeed the Japanese war plan after 1896 envisioned the Russian navy as their principal opponent. Given Japan's ambitious plans for China, Korea, and the rest of Asia, the coming of war with Russia was only a matter of time, particularly after 1902, when the Japanese secured a treaty of alliance with Britain under which each nation pledged to remain neutral in the event of the other going to war with a third power. Further, should any third power side with the enemy of either Britain or Japan, then the other power would join in the partner's defense. This treaty effectively neutralized the Franco-Russian alliance, and in retrospect it is clear that it enabled Japan to pursue her colonial ambitions by going to war with Russia.

5

The Russo-Japanese War

After the Boxer Uprising was quelled, all the partici-
pating nations in the expeditionary force except the
Russians withdrew their troops. The Russians continued to occupy parts of Manchuria. The officials in St.
Petersburg promised to withdraw the troops, but nothing
happened, and it became apparent in Tokyo that Russia and
Japan were travelling on a collision course. The Japanese
Foreign Office made some overtures to the Russians, offer-
ing a tradeoff: the Japanese would ignore the Russian moves
in Manchuria if the Russians would give Japan a free hand
in Korea. But St. Petersburg was not interested in compromise. Her ambitions involved both Korea and Manchuria.

Early in 1902, in preparation for war with Russia, the
Japanese government created a new naval base at Maizuru
on the Sea of Japan, facing Vladivostok. Admiral Togo was
given command of this base. On October 17, 1903, Togo
was summoned to Tokyo and told that war with Russia
seemed inevitable and imminent and that Togo had been
selected to command the fleet.

On December 28 Togo took command and thereupon
began preparing for war. The Japanese fleet was reorganized
into three squadrons, two of which were combined as an

offensive unit. Togo would lead this combined squadron into battle in the flagship *Mikasa*. He was fifty-five years old, but did not look his age. His beard was turning gray at the chin, but the hair on his head was glossy black.

By 1903 the Japanese had developed a superior naval intelligence service, and its reports came to Admiral Togo almost daily from Hong Kong, Manchuria, Korea, and Russia itself, where the Japanese had developed a ring of agents. From these reports Admiral Togo verified his earlier conclusion that the Russian navy was a paper tiger. Many of its ships were outmoded, and many of the new ones did not reach their specified speeds and power.

Still, the Russian navy was the fourth largest in the world, after the British, French, and German. A naval war with Russia involved great risk and enormous expense, a matter of which Admiral Togo was thoroughly aware. Japan had virtually bankrupted her treasury in preparing for this war, with expenditures of 213 million yen, about four times the previous annual expense. If the war were lost the result might even be revolution.

Given this enormous responsibility, Admiral Togo recognized that the solution was to strike first and hard, before the Russian fleet in the west, the preponderant force of the Russian navy, could be brought to Asian waters. This situation dictated a preemptive strike, a matter that Togo discussed with the chief officials of the army, navy, and the Foreign Ministry, who all agreed. Negotiations with the Russians to give Japan a free hand in Korea had failed completely. The decision was made to break off negotiations and strike first, without a declaration of war, and orders were given to Admiral Togo to that effect on February 5, 1904. The next day Togo informed the commanders of his fleet. A few hours later the fleet sailed, at nine o'clock on the morning of February 6.

The plan was simple and straightforward. One element of

the fleet would sail to Korea and attack the Russian ships at Chemulpo and cover the army's landings to occupy Korea. The main body of the fleet would sail straight for Port Arthur and attack the main Russian squadron there. The attack would be carried out on the night of February 8-9 by torpedo boats, and the battle force would attack the next day.

That is how it was done. The torpedo boats attacked just after midnight, and damaged the battleships *Czarevich* and *Revizane* and the heavy cruiser *Pallada*. The following day the major elements of the Japanese fleet attacked the Russian squadron. The attack caused some damage to the Russian fleet, but more to the Japanese, whose major warships were all hit, some of them repeatedly, by Russian fire. The problem was that the Russian squadron remained in the harbor, protected by shore guns and a high hill that prevented the Japanese from getting proper sighting on the ships. Abruptly Admiral Togo broke off the battle and retreated. He had predicted confidently that this battle would decide the outcome of the war, and he had been wrong. The Russian ships had refused to come out to sea and fight.

Even so, the Russian fleet had suffered serious damage and was in no condition to pursue the naval war with the Japanese. To that extent, Admiral Togo had won a qualified victory, and the element that had gone to Korea had destroyed two Russian warships, enabling the Japanese Army to land successfully.

The naval war stumbled along. Togo decided to block Port Arthur by sinking freighters laden with stones across the mouth of the harbor. On February 15 he called for volunteers. Aboard the *Shikishima*, when the call came every man stepped forward. It was the same on all the ships. In the fleet the number of volunteers was twenty times the number of men needed. On February 23 five heavily-laden old ships moved through a calm sea, cheered on by the fighting fleet. The crews sailed into a hail of shot and shell from Russian guns and machine guns. Torpedo boats attacked, trying to divert the Russians, but failed. Only two of the blockships could be scuttled across the harbor mouth; two others ran aground in the shallows near the harbor and the fifth was destroyed by the Russian guns. Frustrated, Admiral Togo ordered a bombardment of the town and the port and for twenty-five minutes the fleet guns thundered and shells fell in Port Arthur, but it was blind firing and not very effective.

At the end of February the word came to Tokyo that Admiral Makarov was coming to Port Arthur to take command. Makarov was the most famous of the Russian admirals. He had made a name for himself by defeating the Turks in the war of 1877, particularly by a daring raid on the port of Batum by night in which he sank several Turkish ships. He had been responsible for a half dozen inventions of naval armament that had been since copied by all nations. And above all, he was a hero of Admiral Togo's, and Togo had caused Makarov's book on tactics to be translated into Japanese and had used it as a text when he was head of the Advanced Naval College.

This war between the Japanese and the Russians had seized the imagination of the world. Every major nation had sent war correspondents to cover the fighting on land and on sea. Here were pitted against each other the "white admiral" and the "yellow admiral". The articles in the press grew ever more sensational as the journalists speculated on the outcome.

Admiral Makarov arrived in Port Arthur on March 6. He flew his flag in the cruiser *Askold*, rather than a battleship, because the *Askold* could make twenty-three knots and was known as the "greyhound of the Russian fleet."

The western correspondents immediately speculated. Who would strike the first blow? Who would win this battle of titans?

Admiral Togo ended the speculation on March 9, when

he launched his fourth attack on Port Arthur. The torpedo boats went in first. This time they met opposition from Makarov's patrols. The fighting was fierce. The Japanese ships met their equals, and sometimes the range was under two hundred yards. But the big Russian ships did not stir from the harbor, and so there was no possibility of a decision.

On March 10 a Russian torpedo boat was cut off by the Japanese Third Squadron. She fought fiercely until her decks were littered with dead, and she could fight no more. The Japanese moved to take the ship in tow, sure of their victory. But two survivors, who had concealed themselves in the engine room of the torpedo boat, opened the sea cocks and scuttled their ship rather than see it captured.

Out from Port Arthur came Admiral Makarov with two cruisers to try to rescue the forlorn torpedo boat, but as they moved to attack the Japanese torpedo boats, the Japanese main fleet moved up, and Admiral Makarov, who was no fool, moved his ships back into the harbor. There was no battle. Instead the Japanese fleet once again shelled Port Arthur blindly.

Admiral Togo's problem that spring was the maintenance of fleet morale when he could not come to grips with the enemy. He had to be ready at any moment for the Russian squadron to try to escape from Port Arthur. He never knew when the attempt would come, so he was forced to keep constant vigilance. It was the most wearing sort of war a vigorous officer could endure.

Day after day the Japanese fleet bombarded Port Arthur. Finally, on March 22, the *Petropavlovsk*, *Sevastopol*, *Pobeda* and *Peresevet* put out to sea. Togo sent the light cruisers to draw the Russian vessels into the open, but they would not take the bait and hugged the coastline. Admiral Makarov was using this foray to train his crews. He was getting ready for a naval battle. But when would he fight? Admiral Togo tried again to force the issue. He ordered another attempt to block the harbor. Again the call for volunteers produced scores more men than could be used. For the second time, the supreme effort was made—the volunteers manned their freighters and took them into the rough hail of Russian fire—but once again they failed to block the harbor.

Admiral Togo now planned a different sort of assault. He would mine the routes the Russians used to get in and out of the harbor, and then make an attack designed to lure them out into the minefield. On April 13 the minefield was completed and Togo brought his fleet up to stage an attack. Admiral Makarov started out of the harbor to respond, but when he saw that he was confronted by six Japanese battleships, four heavy cruisers, and four light cruisers, while he had only two battleships and four cruisers, he turned about to withdraw to the cover of the land batteries. His ships ran into the Japanese minefield as planned, and his flagship, the *Petropavlovsk*, was blown up. The admiral died as his ship went down, thus ending the great battle of wits that the press had built up so forcefully and heightening the tension of the war.

In that same action the *Pobeda* also struck a mine and was seriously damaged, which further reduced the Russian squadron's potential for battle, so that it was almost certain that the Russians would have to send elements of the Western fleet to the Far East.

That spring the Japanese made several more efforts to close up Port Arthur. In one they sent in twelve blockships when a sudden gale blew up and sank all the ships—most of them in advantageous positions. Or so the Japanese thought, since no more Russian ships tried to come out of the harbor. But the real reason was that the new admiral in charge, Admiral Vitheft, had been ordered by St. Petersburg to stop offensive action and wait for reinforcement.

In the ensuing weeks, the Japanese had hard luck. One torpedo boat blew up in a minelaying operation. The *Kasuga*

A Japanese warship under attack during the Russo-Japanese War.

collided with the *Yoshino* and the *Yoshino* sank. The battleship *Yashima* struck a mine and on that same day the battle
ship *Hatsuze* struck another. Both ships sank. The cruiser
Tatzuta, which was picking up survivors, ran aground. In all
eight ships were lost in six days. These disasters and the
impossibility of coming to grips with the enemy might have
destroyed a lesser man, but Admiral Togo seemed unper-
turbed. He remained on course, never missing a detail, never
flinching, and continued to support the army's operations,
waiting, waiting, waiting.

Early on the morning of August 10, the Russian fleet
again prepared to put to sea, and Admiral Togo had received
the message at 6:35 a.m. Togo again prepared for battle.
What he did not know was that Admiral Vitheft had been
ordered to escape to Vladivostok, avoiding battle if it was
possible.

The fleets were soon close enough for accurate gunnery.
The Russians scored first with a twelve-inch shell that hit the
Mikasa's main mast, killing twelve men. Then Vitheft
changed course to port, to avoid the crossing of his T and
trying to pass astern of the Japanese.

Now Togo had a special problem. If he ordered another turn of all his ships simultaneously, the *Mikasa* would move from the head of the line to the end, farthest away from the enemy, and this was the worst possible position for the flagship. So Togo ordered a change of course by the ships turning in succession, which meant the *Mikasa* turned first, and the other ships turned in her wake, following her still. So the Japanese fleet turned west and then north and then east. When the maneuver was finished the two fleets were steaming parallel to each other again, on an easterly course. But in the maneuver, Vitheft had gained ground and was now in the lead, with nothing to bar his way into the open sea of the Gulf of Korea.

At the outset of the war, on the day of the first attack, Admiral Togo had flown a battle flag that said that this was going to be the most important day of the war, but he had been wrong. This day, August 10, was truly a vital day in the history of the Japanese Empire. All might be lost in an hour or two. The admiral's last signal was still aloft on the mast of the *Mikasa*. Make all possible speed, it said.

At 5:30 p.m. Admiral Vitheft realized that he was losing the race, and that he must do something to slow the enemy. His only option was to turn and try to inflict damage on the Japanese. He gave orders then to open fire, and the *Poltava* begin firing her guns. The Battle of the Yellow Sea was joined. Shells began falling around the Japanese ships, and water spouts from them were moving dangerously close. The *Mikasa* took hits on her forecastle and on the bridge. Men and officers were killed, splattering Admiral Togo with their blood.

From the bridge of the *Mikasa* it seemed that the Russian ships had not been hit at all, while several Japanese ships had been damaged. A third of the Japanse heavy twelve-inch guns were out of action already.

Twenty minutes later, Admiral Togo saw a hit on the Russian flagship but it did not seem to slow the ship down. Ten minutes later it seemed that Vitheft had indeed won the race and the battle. Darkness was lowering and Admiral Togo had not stopped the Russian retreat.

But at 6:37 the *Csarevich* began to list and swerved sharply to port. The *Revizane* and the *Pobeda* followed, nearly collided, and then swung back to their original course and steamed in a circle. The *Peresvet* hove to. The Russian fleet action dissolved into confusion, and the Japanese had every advantage. The battle was won. The hit Togo saw on the Russian flagship had blown Admiral Vitheft to pieces. His chief of staff and other officers on the bridge were either killed or wounded. When a second shell exploded at 6:37 it blew up the rest of the bridge, and killed everyone there, put the steering gear of out action, and destroyed the the fire control system. Thus the ship began to steam in a circle and the others followed her. It was minutes before control could be reestablished under the second in command, Prince Oukhtomsky, and a retreat to Port Arthur could begin.

The Russians were bent on escape, and Admiral Togo let them go, apparently not realizing that he could have swooped in for the kill, or perhaps he was so concerned with the future—the coming of the Russian Baltic squadron—that he was not willing to risk a single Japanese vessel to finish off the enemy. In any event the Russians did escape back to Port Arthur, and Admiral Togo never offered any explanation to justify his action in letting them go. The Japanese high command never asked for an explanation. He had won this battle, he had destroyed the Russian leadership of the Pacific squadron, and the *Csarevich* struggled to get to Tsingtao, where she was interned by the Germans. The *Askold* and a torpedo boat put in at Shanghai, where they were interned, and the French interned the *Diana* in Saigon. So for all intents and purposes, the Russian squadron was dispersed and might as well have been destroyed. Togo's eye was on the future. It was the war he was concerned about, not any single battle. He knew that he had to conserve every ship to fight the big battle that was coming up against the Russian Baltic squadron.

Meanwhile, the Japanese army took a hand. General Nogi had been fighting his way across Manchuria and finally reached Port Arthur. After a long and arduous struggle against the most heroic Russian army resistance, at the end of November the Japanese captured the key positions around the harbor, including High Mountain Hill, and from there they were able to train their artillery on the Russian fleet. In a matter of hours the *Poltava* was sunk, and the *Revizane* and the *Peresvet* were sunk and then the *Pobeda* and the *Pallada*. The *Sevastopol* was attacked by Japanese torpedo boats and ran aground, and the Russian Pacific squadron was at last wiped out.

Only then could Admiral Togo return to Japan with his own squadron for a refit and repairs to his damaged ships. On December 30, 1904, he arrived in Tokyo, greeted by an adoring crowd of hundreds of thousands on his way to see the emperor. When he met the crowd, the admiral took off his cap, and those who knew him saw that since he had last been in the capital, his hair had turned as white as snow.

6

The Battle of Tsushima Strait

Admiral Togo had an audience with Emperor Meiji on that day of his arrival back in Japan, and then took leave for just three days. There was no time for more, because the specter of the Russian Baltic Fleet, now called the Second Pacific squadron, hung over all Japan. General Nogi was winning the war on the land in Manchuria in spite of the stout defenses of the Russians. The Imperial Army was boastfully beginning to create the myth of Japanese military invincibility. But Admiral Togo knew better. Japan was winning in Manchuria because her supply lines were shorter than the Russians'. That was true only because Admiral Togo's fleet dominated the seas. If the fleet were to be defeated by the Russians, the military situation would quickly be reversed, and Japan would lose the war. Despite all the jingoist propaganda that flooded Japan, Admiral Togo never lost sight of that salient fact. Togo's life ashore that winter consisted of one conference after another. He reorganized the Imperial Navy, with specific emphasis on the fighting fleet. He promoted his chief of staff, Admiral Shimamura, to command of a fighting division, and brought in Rear Admiral Kato as his new staff chief. He spent many hours planning for the battle on which the fate of the Empire would truly depend. For more than a year he had imposed his discipline on the Japanese fleet and the men had responded willingly to forge a thoroughly integrated organization. The high command had given him everything for which he had asked. He had the largest and best vessels the Japanese government could afford. Now his organization and his ships were to be tested.

As Admiral Togo planned, Japan's naval shipyards were abuzz with activity in the rebuilding of the Imperial Fleet. The ships had gone for months without proper maintenance, and even battle damage had not been repaired. But now engines, guns, and hulls were refitted and sometimes rebuilt. The fleet's charts were revised and a whole new system of plotting was devised. The charts were overprinted with grid squares, which made it easy to place any ship that was reporting. New signal stations were set up all around Japan, and new wireless stations established.

Putting himself in the position of Admiral Rojestvensky, his opponent in the coming battle, Admiral Togo had to draw several conclusions and act on them. Where would the Russian fleet base itself? He decided that the only sensible answer was Vladivostok, and his plans were set accordingly.

And where would the fateful encounter take place? Togo considered three possibilities:

1. Admiral Rojestvensky could steam around Japan to the east and come through LaPerouse Strait between Hokkaido and Sakhalin islands. But this narrow strait was easy to mine, and could only be reached after running the gauntlet of the Kurils and their reefs. No admiral in his right mind would choose that route.

2. The Russians might come through the Tsugaru Narrows, between Hokkaido and Honshu. But this strait was also very narrow, could easily be mined, and was swept by very strong tidal currents. Besides, it was flanked by Japanese naval bases. In fact, it was already mined, and Admiral

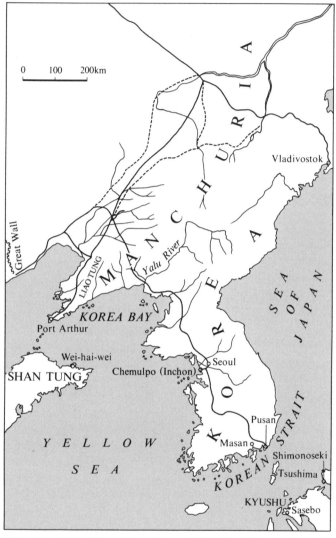

China, Manchuria, Korea, Japan (Area of Blockade of Port Arthur and Battle of Tsushima Strait)

Togo had to assume that the Russians knew it.

3. The enemy might choose the Strait of Korea, which was much more open and much less dangerous than the other two approaches. It could not be successfully mined, as at one hundred miles across it was much too broad.

Admiral Togo concluded that Admiral Rojestvensky would use the Strait of Korea, and thereafter he based his battle plan on that assumption, and based his vessels accordingly. The main body of the fleet was to be moved to Masan on the southern coast of Korea near the Tsushima Strait. The cruisers were to be based at Osaki, on Tsushima island in the middle of the strait.

Japan's naval intelligence network had been aware of the Russian plans to send the Baltic Fleet to the Pacific since its inception the year before. Admiral Togo knew that the Baltic squadron consisted of the cream of the Russian aristocracy, most of whose sons chose the more glamorous naval service over the army. For many weeks, as the fleet prepared to sail, the officers had been feasted and entertained at banquets and balls, in which the uppermost level of Russian society had participated. The sailing of the fleet was a joyous occasion, in which the naval officer corps promised faithfully to revenge the dastardly, unprovoked attack on Port Arthur by the Japanese. Western newspapers were full of the boasts of the Russian commanders, and indeed the Western world anticipated a Russian victory in the battle to come and a turn-around in the Russo-Japanese War.

It was true that Admiral Rojestvensky had never commanded a fleet in battle, but that was not his fault. Russia had not engaged in a modern war, but like every other navy she had been preparing for one. In the speculations in Western military circles, the Russians were given the edge over the Japanese in naval strength, despite several vital considerations. The Japanese were more experienced, having fought the Chinese only a few years before, and then having fought

the Russian Pacific squadron for the past year. But five of
the Russians' seven battleships were new and their gunnery
equipment was the finest that could be obtained, although
the Japanese had equal equipment and much more experience in using it. In communications the Russian fleet was
deficient, because someone in the supply department had
decided to save money and refused to buy the latest Marconi
wireless equipment, which the Japanese had installed eager-
ly as soon as it was available. But this was not generally
known to the outside world and as the Russian fleet of forty
ships set out it looked very formidable indeed. Most important, it had eight battleships all told, to Admiral Togo's four,
and in those days battleships were what the world liked to
count. The fact that Togo had eight cruisers to the Russian
two was not considered very important.

When the Russian fleet had set sail from Reval in the
Gulf of Finland in October, it headed up through the North
Sea, around Scotland and the Dogger Bank to enter the
Atlantic for its voyage around the world. The depot ship
Kamchatka, steaming behind the fighting fleet, suddenly
announced by wireless that it was being attacked by torpedo
boats. Then rockets were sighted near the fleet. The entire
Russian fleet was alerted and began firing that continued for
about twelve minutes, when someone realized that no one
was firing back. Ultimately it was discovered that the alarm
had been set off when the *Kamchatka* had passed through
the Hull trawler fleet, which was setting out for its fishing
grounds. One trawler was sunk and many fishermen were
killed and wounded by the reckless display, which caused a
worldwide reaction, and cost the Russian government a large
sum in reparation.

In the investigation that followed, the Russian high command placed the blame for the incident on officers in the
fleet who had started a rumor that the Japanese had been
buying up small vessels in the North Sea and were planning

to attack the fleet before it reached the Atlantic.

In spite of this ridiculous incident, the appearance of the Russian fleet was impressive as it made its difficult way around the world. On December 19 the fleet reached the Cape of Good Hope. A few days later, when the fleet was anchored for a break off Madagascar, Admiral Rojestvensky learned that the Russian defenders of Port Arthur had just surrendered. The news was a blow, but the admiral believed that the defeat on land could be retrieved by a victory at sea. On April 8, 1905, the squadron passed through the Strait of Malacca and by Singapore. The Western press was loud in the praises of the Russsians for having carried out such a magnificent feat, sailing 16,000 miles without touching any base. Now the fleet was approaching its target and entering the China Sea. Within twenty-four hours, Admiral Togo knew where his enemy was. He also knew that the Russian sailing was sloppy, the ships did not keep station properly, that the battleships were so heavily laden with supplies that their decks were awash, and that their color scheme of dark gray hulls and yellow funnels made excellent targets.

On April 14, Japanese agents in Indo-China reported that the Russians had anchored in Cam Ranh Bay on the Indo-China coast and were carrying out fleet exercises. On May 13, Togo learned that Rojestvensky had been joined by a fourth Russian squadron from the Baltic. Five days later Japanese agents reported that fifty ships had sailed on a northerly course. That was the last Togo heard from his agents. Now he had to estimate when his enemy would arrive in Japanese waters.

On the evening of May 26, 1905, the Japanese fleet lay at anchor at Masan: Togo's four battleships, two new heavy cruisers, Admiral Kamimura's cruiser force, Admiral Uryu's cruiser force and a large number of torpedo boats. At Osaki lay Admiral Kataoka's cruisers. At sea, cruisers and auxiliary cruisers watched for the enemy, whose presence was expected momentarily.

At 2:45 on the morning of May 27 the expanded Russian fleet arrived. The auxiliary cruiser *Shinano Maru* sighted the Russian battle line, and shortly afterward sent off a message to Admiral Togo announcing that the Russians seemed to be steering for the western passage past Tsushima Island.

At 5:05 in the morning Admiral Togo received the message, and less than an hour later the flagship put to sea at the head of the Japanese line of battle. The *Mikasa* was first in line, then the *Shikishima*, the *Fuji*, *Asahi*, *Kasuga*, *Nichine*— four battleships and two heavy cruisers in all. Togo moved to meet the Russians at two o'clock in the afternoon near the island of Okinoshima.

An artist's conception of the deck of Admiral Togo's flagship, the *Mikasa*, during the Battle of Tsushima Strait.

At 11 in the morning came the news that the Russians had opened fire on the cruisers of Admiral Dewa, but that Dewa had not fired back and had withdrawn from range. This was the result of Russian nervousness. The *Orel* had accidentally fired a gun, and the whole fleet had begun firing. As soon as Admiral Rojestvensky learned of this he had stopped this waste of ammunition. Here again was an indication of the state of Russian fire discipline.

Admiral Togo had conceived a complicated battle plan, starting with a torpedo boat attack and extending over four days, but the weather and the actions of the Russians dictated a major change. The weather was so rough that the torpedo boats had to stay in port, and the two battle fleets were drawing together, so the first action would involve the battleships.

At 1:15 in the afternoon the *Mikasa* sighted Admiral Dewa's cruisers, which were shadowing the enemy, and a little later Togo saw the yellow funnels and dark hulls of the Russian battle fleet.

At 1:55 the *Mikasa* ran up the admiral's battle flag:

"The country's fate depends upon this battle," it read, "Let every man do his duty with all his might."

The Russians were steaming in two columns, with the biggest ships, the *Suvarov*, *Alexander III*, *Borodino*, and *Orel* on the starboard, and the *Oslabia* leading the second line. The Russians were steaming north, obviously heading for Vladivostok. Togo would stop them by attacking from the west.

At the moment the two fleets were steaming directly toward each other, Togo ordered a change to port, in succession, which meant that every ship followed the one ahead of it and turned at the same point. This presented the Russians with a whole succession of targets, one by one, and when Rojestvensky saw what Togo was doing he thought the Japanese admiral had lost his senses to give the enemy such an advantage. At 2:08 the turning began, the Russians opened fire, and the air around the Japanese ships was filled with exploding shells. But the Japanese held to course and did not fire back. The maneuver took three minutes, and then the Japanese ships also began to fire.

A shell exploded aboard the *Mikasa*, wounding fifteen officers standing behind the bridge, and smashing the compass next to where Togo was standing. He did not stir. A few minutes later one of the flagship's guns was hit.

But by then the turn was completed; the Japanese had the advantage and the Japanese gunners were finding the range. For more than half an hour the fleets steamed parallel to each other, and the Japanese gunners scored many hits. By 3 p.m. Togo had moved to cross the Russian T and bar the way to Vladivostok. The Japanese were using a new armor-piercing shell of great power and effectiveness, and they were blasting the Russian ships to pieces, firing at a rate three times as fast as the enemy, an indication of their superior training and weaponry. Within that first half-hour, the Russian effectiveness had been destroyed, their rangefinders and fire control apparatus were wrecked, and they began firing wildly, while the Japanese scored hit after hit. The decks of the Russian vessels were literally covered with blood and parts of bodies.

At 2:47 the Japanese were steering east southeast and the range was only 4500 yards. At 2:50 the *Oslabia*, surrounded by black smoke, withdrew from the battle. Ten minutes later the *Suvarov* was afire from one end to the other, and she also quit the fight. The *Alexander III* suddenly altered course and headed for Vladivostok. The Japanese turned and again barred the way.

At 3:10 the *Oslabia* capsized and sank. Admiral Kamimura's cruisers were concentrating their fire on the *Alexander III*. The *Borodino* was in flames. The Japanese turned again and continued to hammer the Russian fleet. The

Suvarov, out of control, was burning briskly, hit from one side by Kamimura's cruisers and from the other by Togo's battleships. The Russian rate of fire slowed and then almost stopped, as the Russian ships milled about senselessly in between the Japanese firing lines. By this time the *Suvarov* was reduced to firing one three-inch gun, and drifting almost helplessly. She had been the center of the Japanese fleet's attention for hours and was now a hopeless wreck, but she fought on. Admiral Togo ordered Commander Fujimoto's torpedo boat flotilla to attack her. The torpedo boats attacked, but still she resisted. Not until the torpedo boats had made three attacks and torpedoed her repeatedly did the *Suvarov* slowly settle, and then sink.

As she went down a violent explosion shook the *Borodino*, which was trying to rally the remnants of the Russian fleet and lead the ships toward Vladivostok. The ship vanished from the surface. The *Alexander III* went down with all her crew; not a man survived. The *Kamchatka*, *Ural*, and *Russ* were sunk by gunfire. Two hospital ships were captured.

Now the Russian fleet had been disorganized and major elements sunk. It was time for a night torpedo attack to carry out the next part of the plan, and night was approaching. Togo ordered a cease fire. The Japanese battle line headed north, and made plans for an assembly of the fleet at sea in the morning off Matsushima.

He then assessed the results for the day. The Japanese fleet had a hundred men killed and 530 wounded. The *Mikasa* had been the main target of the Russians and she had been hit forty-eight times. Only five of her six-inch guns were intact. The big guns were all silenced. The *Nichine* had also suffered serious damage, and Admiral Misu, in command, had been wounded. The *Asama* was half under water but still on station, the *Kassagin* had left the battle with a large hole in her hull and gone into the bay of Aburadani, and other ships had been damaged but none were in danger of sinking.

In exchange for this damage, Togo had sunk three of the four new *Suvarov* class battleships, which were supposed to be unsinkable, and many other vessels.

The Russians stopped up the leaks in their ships, pulled their armament together, and hoped for a better day in the morning. Perhaps they could reach Vladivostok. The Japanese had stopped firing, and the lights of their ships had vanished in the darkness.

But the hope lasted for only an hour, then the sea was again filled with the noise of engines as the Japanese torpedo boats came in to make their attack. They charged straight into the beams of the Russian searchlights, launching torpedoes, and then turned, sped out and came in again as long as they had torpedoes to fire.

The battleship *Navarin* was hit twice and sank with nearly all hands. The battleship *Sissoy Velsky* and the cruiser *Admiral Nakimov* managed to make the shore of Tsushima Island, where their crews scuttled them to avoid capture.

But other ships fought on, and the Russian gunners, many of them wounded and bandaged, managed their guns skillfully. They sank two Japanese torpedo boats and put six others out of the fight before it ended in the withdrawal of the torpedo boats as dawn began to come up.

The day dawned bright and sunny, the weather Admiral Togo needed for the next part of his plan. The Imperial Fleet deployed in a wide fan and began to sweep the sea in the direction of Matsushima. At 5:20 Togo had word of the first sighting of the enemy. Admiral Kataoka's Fifth Division had seen the smoke of the enemy sixty miles to Togo's south. A few minutes later came more news. The force consisted of four enemy battleships and several other ships, heading northwest, trying to reach Vladivostok. Togo again headed up to cross the enemy course, and cap the T. This time the conditions were perfect. His First and Second Divisions would intercept the enemy and the Fourth, Fifth, and Sixth Divisions would harry him from the south.

Just after 10 a.m. the Russian fleet came in sight. The old *Nicholas I*, flying a command flag, was leading the line, followed by the *Orel* and two other armored ships, the *Apraxine* and the *Seniavine*. The cruiser *Izumrud* was steaming abeam of the line.

At 10:30 the *Kasuga* opened fire, and all the other Japanese battleships began firing. The *Izumrud* left the battle and steered due east to escape. She was followed by the *Chitose*, but the Japanese ship was losing the race.

The other Russian ships could not escape. They were encircled and under heavy fire. Then the admiral's flag aboard the *Nicholas I* was dropped to half-mast and the signal code XGH was run up. The Russians were asking to negotiate. Togo ignored the Russian signal. The other Russian ships began striking their colors, and ran up the Rising Sun flag of Japan. They were surrendering. Togo did nothing. His officers looked at him,

"Should we cease fire?" one staff officer asked.

Togo was still silent and the Japanese guns were still firing on the surrendered Russian ships.

"Should we not stop firing?" came the question another time.

Still it was met by silence.

Then one of the officers insisted.

"Does not the spirit of *bushido* require that we cease fire?"

Admiral Togo remembered his past and his obligations and ordered his fleet to cease fire.

Togo sent an officer to board the *Nicholas I* and bring Admiral Rojestvensky aboard the Japanese flagship, but the admiral was not aboard. Wounded, and only half-conscious, he was aboard the torpedo boat *Byedovi*. Rear Admiral

Nebogatov was in charge. He donned his dress uniform with medals and went aboard the *Mikasa* to be told the conditions of surrender: the ships were to be handed over to the Japanese as they were, the crews would become prisoners of war, and the officers could keep their swords and would be paroled. When Nebogatov asked what treatment the crews would receive, Togo answered curtly that the Japanese were not barbarians.

The greatest naval battle of the century was over. The Russians had lost 4,830 men killed, while the Japanese had lost 117. Thousands of Russians had been wounded, and a thousand Japanese. The Russian fleet no longer existed; the Japanese fleet had lost only three torpedo boats. Of the entire Russian armada, only one cruiser and two destroyers reached Vladivostok. All the rest were sunk, interned by neutrals, or captured.

A few weeks after the battle of Tsushima Japanese naval vessels escorted ships carrying the Thirteenth Army Division from Sasebo to join the war. For the defense of Harbin and Vladivostok the Russians could now use only the Trans-Siberian Railroad, and there was nothing to interfere with the Japanese at sea. The war on land turned around now that the war at sea was won. European nations began to express concern about Japan's ambitions. The Americans offered their services as intermediaries to end the war, and Russia and Japan both accepted. Russia was erupting in rebellion following the destruction of the fleet, and Japan was nearly bankrupted by the war expenditures.

Japan had won a victory and new respect from the world, but it was a very expensive one.

7

The Hero of Japan

In victory, Admiral Togo was the perfect hero. He and all his senior commanders were greeted by the emperor, who congratulated them on their victory. He was feted by the nation. An army of celebrated poets composed odes, which they read at a public ceremony in his honor. Everywhere he was followed by cheering crowds. He stood beside the emperor at the naval review held at Yokohama where eight battleships, twelve heavy cruisers and light cruisers, twenty-eight destroyers, seventy-seven torpedo boats, and five new submarines steamed past, their guns thundering in salute. He honored and lamented his dead heroes in a ceremony at Aoyama Cemetery in Tokyo.

On December 20, 1905, Admiral Togo was appointed chief of the Imperial General Staff and on this occasion he gave a warning to his country in the fashion he had learned as a young samurai:

"The gods award the crown to those who, by their training in peacetime, are victorious even before they go into battle," he said. "But the gods soon take the crown away from those who relax in the pleasures of peace." And he quoted an adage of the samurai: "After a victory, tighten your helmet."

Admiral Togo served as chief of the Imperial General

71

Staff from December 1905 to December 1909. The clouds of war never really gathered again over Japan during his lifetime although the seeds of a new war were sprouting. American President Theodore Roosevelt, who interceded in the negotiations between Japan and Russia at the Treaty of Portsmouth, pulled the Russians' chestnuts out of the fire. Japan had been demanding a large cash indemnity to restore the national treasury after the enormous expenses of the war. Roosevelt pointed out that the Japanese had started the war, and prevented them from getting the indemnity, to the fury of the Japanese military establishment and much of the Japanese public. Togo and other military leaders then began to eye the United States with a new suspicion that was reciprocated, and exacerbated by growing racism in the United States. President Roosevelt became convinced that Japan was now a definite threat to Anglo-American domination of the Pacific, and the Japanese rapidly became convinced that America was the prime threat to Japanese ambitions to become the leader of Asia.

The mutual suspicion was magnified ten times over when Roosevelt sent the U.S. Navy's principal combat vessels on a "Good Will Tour" of the world. It was obvious that the purpose of the tour was to visit Australia, the Philippines, Japan, and China, as a warning to Japan. By the time the "Great White Fleet" reached Australia in 1908, the people of the United States, Australia, New Zealand, and Japan all erupted in convolutions of jingoism, the Westerners in anti-Japanese demonstrations, and the people of Japan in anti-western feeling. Togo organized a greeting for the bellicose Americans. As they neared Japan the entire Imperial Fleet—160 ships—sailed out to meet and escort the Americans into Japanese waters. The fleets did not meet, and a typhoon smashed up the demonstrations, but the implications were all too clear. Admiral Togo knew who his new enemies would be, and he planned accordingly.

The Japanese war plan thus selected a new potential enemy, the United States, and the naval war plans and exercises each year were directed against the U.S. The Americans reciprocated by drawing up Plan Orange, the plan for the U.S. Navy's war against Japan, and from that time the two nations moved slowly but steadily toward war.

In 1911 Admiral Togo joined General Nogi and the Prince and Princess Higashi-Fushimi of the royal family in representing Japan at the coronation of King George V in London. He joined the king in a review of the Royal Navy at Spithead and he visited his old training ships, and now "Johnny Chinaman" was now received with honors and addressed the naval cadets.

On his retirement from the service Togo and General Nogi were chosen by the Emperor Meiji to supervise the education of his grandson, Prince Hirohito, who was expected to succeed to the throne. In samurai fashion, Nogi and his wife committed suicide upon the death of the emperor in 1912, but Togo continued to watch over Hirohito's education until 1920, when the prince attained his majority. He inculcated a respect for the British that was extended when Hirohito visited England that year and stayed at Buckingham Palace.

As regards America, that drift toward war was hardly ameliorated by the intrusion of World War I. The Japanese, called by their obligation under the Japanese-British alliance, went to war with Germany, while the United States maintained a stubborn neutrality and viewed Japan's assault on Kiaochao and the other German colonies of the Pacific as a manifestation of Lord Hatta's policy for Japan to lie low and move in on Asia while the rest of the world was distracted. The suspicions of America were scarcely allayed by the newfound alliance in 1917, when the United States entered the war and Japan and the U.S. jointly engaged in the occupation of Siberia. They were increased in the postwar period

Admiral Togo (front row, third from left) together with other leading members of the Imperial Navy.

by Japan's fortification of her League of Nations mandates in the Pacific. Then, when Japanese militarists came into power in the 1930s and Japan was turned into an armed camp, the drift became pronounced; war with China capped it and set the scene for the great Pacific War.

In all this, Admiral Togo was a fervent advocate of stout national defense and national expansion, although he never came out flatly in favor of the militarization of the country, and his disciples were on both sides of the navy's quarrel over treaty limitations on the Japanese navy in the 1920s and early 1930s. He limited his statements to naval affairs, but here he joined the aggressive Fleet faction of the navy and became their strongest advocate.

When he died in 1934 he was given the first state funeral ever accorded a man who was not at least a prince of royal blood. He was buried in Tama cemetery, thirty-five miles from Tokyo.

Togo was never one to talk much about his ideas, and in his last years he was retired from public life and more inclined to consider the roses in his garden than the national military budget. His legacies to the Japanese military were many and as the 21st century neared they continued. His legacy of the samurai, to win first and fight later, was adopted by Admiral Isoroku Yamamoto in staging the Pearl Harbor attack on the United States Navy. His strict discipline and insistence on perfectionism in organization and performance continued in the days of the Imperial Navy, and the legacy has been handed on to the Japanese Naval Defense Force. His awareness of the need for modern methods and logical thinking guided the building of Japan's modern navy and was continued through the service academies.

Admiral Togo's reputation was tarnished at the end of World War II when the defeat of Japan brought a revulsion against all things military. References to his military activities were sharply curtailed in school textbooks and his name epitomized all the evils of militarism. The anniversaries of his birth and death went unremarked for many years. Only at the end of the 1980s was Togo rehabilitated and a new statue to his memory erected in Satsuma.

His greatest single claim to fame is so enormous that it is difficult to express. He was the one man who led Japan's navy forces into a modern world that for a time it dominated, and he bequeathed to the Japanese naval tradition the philosophy that victory in battle is everything.

Isoroku Yamamoto

Admiral Isoroku Yamamoto.

1

Isoroku Yamamoto and
the New Navy

Like Admiral Togo, the man who would be Admiral Yamamoto was born into a samurai family. He was the child of his father's second marriage and he was named Isoroku—literally "Fifty-six"—because his father was fifty-six years old at the time of the boy's birth in 1884. Isoroku's family name was not Yamamoto, but Takano. His father had fought for the shogunate in the wars that led to the modernization of Japan, which meant that he and his family received no favors from the new Meiji government, and so after the wars Sadayoshi Takano made a meager living as a swordmaker in Nagaoka, Niigata, in the mountainous north of Honshu island.

Early in life Isoroku came under the influence of American missionaries. His first school was a mission school where he studied the Bible and the English language. He did not become a Christian but the influence on him was lasting. He continued his study of English at the Nagaoka Middle School under a teacher named Newall. Some days after school, he went to the house of Mr. Newall to drink coffee and practice his English.

In 1901 Isoroku took an examination for admission to the Imperial Naval Academy at Eta Jima. He placed high on the list and was appointed, in spite of the family history (the Meiji government was now trying to heal the old wounds of civil war and promote national unity) and he entered the academy that year.

At the academy he was almost alone in his respect for things Western. Even after years of indoctrination with the British naval tradition it was apparent that Westernization was only technical and superficial. By this time the influence of Admiral Togo and the others who had been personally exposed to a British naval education had been fully felt, and so it must be presumed that the negative feelings about the West were deliberately fostered in the Japanese establishment. The anti-Western feeling of the general population was already showing itself in demonstrations throughout the country. All the other cadets were insular Japanese with strong xenophobic attitudes. Once, when they discovered Isoroku reading his Bible, they taunted him for being a foreigner-lover, whereupon he lectured them on the need to understand the West and to learn from Westerners the secrets of their technological superiority. Having explained his position with great good humor he threw the delegation out of his room and went back to reading his Bible.

Isoroku graduated from the naval academy in the spring of 1904 as a gunnery specialist. After a brief training ship cruise he was assigned to the cruiser *Nisshin*, and soon was involved in the operations of the Imperial Navy in the Russo-Japanese War. In the spring of 1905 the Russian Baltic fleet appeared in Asian waters and the Battle of Tsushima Strait was fought. During the battle Sublieutenant Takano was wounded, either by the explosion of an enemy shell near his battle station or the bursting of one of the *Nisshin*'s guns. He was wounded in the leg and lost the index finger and second finger of his left hand. He spent several months in the hospital, during which he received a letter of commendation from Admiral Togo, which was to prove valuable to his career.

In three months Isoroku was back on duty. His career then followed the normal lines of an Imperial Navy officer: slow but steady promotion, to lieutenant and then to lieutenant commander. As a student of America and the English language, Isoroku in these years watched with growing concern the deterioration of Japanese-American relations.

As already noted, the problem had really begun in 1906 with the Treaty of Portsmouth, which ended the Russo-Japanese War. Isoroku did not share the general resentment of the Japanese military against Westerners, perhaps because of his early exposure to American missionaries. He continued to have a respect for the West, a respect that increased as his English improved. In 1913 he was appointed to the Naval Staff College in Tokyo, a prerequisite for promotion to the higher reaches of the navy. That same year, after completing the course, he served as gunnery officer aboard the battleship *Shintaku*.

In 1916 Isoroku was adopted into the Yamamoto family of Nagaoka. This was not an unusual act in Japan. Admiral Gonnohyoe Yamamoto was the last surviving male of a distinguished line of Japanese naval officers and samurai and the family wanted the name to survive.

Three years later Lieutenant Commander Yamamoto was selected to spend two years of study in the United States, to further perfect his command of the English language. (It was also expected that he would learn as much about America as possible.) He was sent to Harvard University, where he had plenty of leisure and took every opportunity to travel around America, observing American industry, oil production and other matters that interested the Navy. (He also became an adept bridge player.) In 1920 he visited Detroit, where he was enormously impressed by the productivity of the automobile industry, and went to Mexico and Texas to visit the oil fields. He became convinced that for the Japanese to seek war with America would be absolutely suicidal, given the American industrial capacity and Japan's own dearth of resources.

In the 1920s the Imperial Navy separated into two factions. In the naval disarmament treaty signed in Washington in 1922, the Japanese agreed to a limitation of naval armament with a ratio of three ships to five each for the United States and Britain. The treaty was negotiated for Japan by Navy Minister Admiral Tomosaburo Kato. Admiral Kanji Kato took violent exception to the treaty, as did Admiral Togo and many other elder members of the Japanese naval establishment, who believed that Japan had a mission to lead East Asia out of colonialism and assume leadership in the Asia of the future. That involved pushing Westerners entirely out of Asia. This aggressive naval faction came to be known as the Fleet faction, and it took a defiantly expansionist stand. The other faction of the navy, to which Yamamoto subscribed, was the Treaty faction, which held that war with the U.S. was unthinkable. The Navy thus divided along the same lines as the army, which split into the Action and Control factions. The former, led by several generals, demanded expansion of the Japanese empire and control by the army of Japanese affairs. The latter wanted international cooperation and an end to empire building. The struggle between these factions for control of Japanese military and naval policy continued quietly all through the 1920s, but would break out in the 1930s in violence directed at the civil authorities by the activist military and naval leaders against civilian control.

In 1922 Commander Yamamoto accompanied Admiral Kenji Ide on a trip to Europe to examine the navies of that region. It involved ceremonial visits to England, France, Italy, Austria, Germany, and once more to America. While they were on the trip, Yamamoto was promoted to the rank of captain in the Imperial Navy. He was soon appointed captain of the cruiser *Fuji*. But Yamamoto's mind was turning to military aviation, certainly stimulated by the Billy Mitchell controversy over the role of air power that raged in the United States in the 1920s, and the Washington Naval Conference, which made an exception for aircraft carriers in the limitation of ships. Yamamoto believed that aviation was the navy's future, and in the fall of 1924 he managed to get appointed to a job that put him in the middle of the growing aviation field—executive officer of the Kasumigaura Aviation Corps school. Aviation was only three years old in the Japanese navy at that time. The fact that Yamamoto was a line officer, not a pilot, did not matter. He was not expected to fly, but to instill naval discipline into the school. But Yamamoto intended to be the complete airman, and although he was forty years old he set out to learn to fly and to master aeronautics. He delayed his assumption of official duties while he trained and studied. By the end of the year he was a competent aviator, and then he took over as executive officer and director of studies of the school.

In 1925 Captain Yamamoto was posted to Washington as naval attache at the Japanese Embassy, and there he became very familiar with the American navy. He made it a point to play bridge with American naval officers, with the larger objective of learning how they thought and made decisions. All that he learned confirmed his belief that Japan must at all costs avoid confrontation with the United States, and after his tour of duty ended in 1928, he went back to Japan to use his influence to maintain peaceful relations.

2

The Rising Star

Captain Yamamoto was next placed in command of the aircraft carrier *Akagi*, which had just joined the fleet as flagship of the carrier force. As captain he was deeply involved in one of Japan's early aeronautical tragedies. In January 1929, while on maneuvers off the China coast, he sent his planes to attack "the enemy." They got lost in the increasingly bad weather, and all of them crashed in the sea. None of the fliers was ever found. Yamamoto was profoundly affected by this incident and forever after he placed a very high value on human life, a characteristic that was not shared by many of his fellow naval officers.

By 1929 it was apparent that Yamamoto, then forty-five, would become an admiral. For one thing he was Japan's foremost naval expert on America. For another, he was a master of technology, and knew more about the workings of a carrier and the air arm than any other Japanese naval officer. And finally, he was most competent in the use of the English language. So when a delegation was appointed to go to London in 1930 to negotiate a new naval treaty with the British and the Americans, Captain Yamamoto was chosen as a special assistant to accompany it. During the journey to England he was promoted to rear admiral.

The London Naval Confereence of 1930 was called because the earlier Washington Conference had failed to establish any limits for all vessels. Britain, the United States, and Japan had been building all types of unrestricted ships, cruisers and submarines in particular, to the point that if the trend continued the limitation on battleships and carriers would soon be meaningless.

When the conference was organized the Japanese government had indicated its intention of seeking a change in the 5-5-3 ratio that gave Japan only three-fifths of the naval armament of America and Britain. An interim conference called at Geneva in 1927 had failed when the United States and Britain could not agree on a limit for cruisers. Japan had tried to play a conciliatory role at those meetings, but the other two powers would not budge from their positions, the Americans holding out for a number of heavy cruisers for fleet purposes and the British wanting many light cruisers to meet the needs of their empire. The Japanese aim at that conference had been to increase their country's ratio to seventy percent of the others, but the discussions never got that far. The Americans were totally unyielding. To save face the participants announced a temporary recess.

Japan's position as put forward by Admiral Makoto Saito had been conciliatory; the Admiral recognized that Japan's economic strength, much weakened after the European War of 1914-18 and the subsequent economic inflation, would not permit her to engage in an arms race. Furthermore, he announced that Japan had to consider her vital needs and ignore the ambitions of a group of naval officers who were pressing for Japanese expansion to the point of control of Asian waters.

"Bluffing is inadvisable," Saito warned this group. "It won't do. The only way to attain both safety and expansion is to stick to our present position. Our nation's power will increase, our economic strength, our industrial strength, our sense of honor, and our international morality will be increasingly understood and respected by the world. Gradually the nation's power will grow strong. In other words, we must refrain from acting like automatons and trying to increase our naval strength by means of one or two conferences. We will not be able to get them to sit down at a desk and hurriedly write us out a promissory note."

After the failure of the Geneva conference, naval power again became a major issue in the United States. In January 1928 the United States Congress received a plan from the navy for an enormous expansion of the fleet, including twenty-five heavy cruisers, thirty-two submarines, and five aircraft carriers. Only when the British announced that they were eliminating some increases in their budget did the forces of limitation in American manage to reduce the navy's big plans. In 1928 the Americans and British worked hard to reduce their areas of friction and made much progress. But in Japan events were taking a different turn.

When the Japanese delegation had set out for Geneva in 1927 a new cabinet headed by General Giichi Tanaka had come to power in Japan. The Tanaka cabinet represented primarily the Imperial Army's as yet somewhat inchoate ambitions for expansion of empire, and Tanaka began to work to wrench Manchuria away from China. He took a trip to Manchuria and in Mukden made a speech to officers of the Kwantung Army calling for the takeover of Manchuria. The speech was leaked to a Shanghai newspaper and published as "The Tanaka Memorandum." The Japanese government called it a fake but its statement of army policy was real. The affair aroused so much controversy in the world that Tanaka was forced to resign after the army took the first step, the assassination of Manchurian warlord Chang Tso-lin (Zhang Zolin). The new cabinet of Prime Minister Osachi Hamaguchi was dedicated to reform of the aggressive China policy of the past, arms reduction, budget limitation, and reform of education. One of the cabinet's first steps was to set sharp limits on military spending.

The Japanese delegates to the London Conference of 1930 were led by former Prime Minister Reijiro Wakatsuki, Navy Minister Takeshi Takarabe, with Admiral Kiyokami Abe and Vice Admiral Seizo Sakoniji as senior advisors. They went to London with a 10-10-7 ratio in mind (the figure authorized by the cabinet). At the opening of the conference Wakatsuki said that Japan wanted to go beyond ratios to the actual reduction of arms. Japan was interested in having forces capable of defense but not aggression.

But the navy split into Treaty and Fleet factions right in the middle of the conference. The Treaty Faction held that the Tokyo guidelines should be sought but not insisted upon. The Fleet Faction set seventy percent as the absolute minimum.

Several new problems arose in London. The British wanted to outlaw the submarine. For quite different reasons the Japanese and Americans disagreed. The Japanese saw the submarine as a purely military weapon, the eyes of the fleet and a counterfoil against the battleship and cruiser. The Americans saw the submarine (as did the Germans) as a strategic weapon for the destruction of commerce and thus the enemy's industrial power. So the Japanese and Americans combined forces to overwhelm the British and prevent the elimination of the submarine.

The British wanted a moratorium on battleship construction. The Japanese knew that the British had many battleships, some of them started in World War I, while Japan had few. They opposed this moratorium and the American supported them. After much discussion the Americans agreed to a quota almost reaching the seventy percent figure the Japanese wanted and the delegates asked Tokyo for advice. When the assistant navy minister asked for the opinions of the senior admirals of the fleet, he precipitated a factional fight without precedence in the Japanese Navy. The Fleet faction would not budge. Admiral Kanji Kato was the most obdurate; if the Japanese did not get exactly what they wanted, he said, they should withdraw from the conference.

If Japan's demands broke up the conference, he added, then "the puritans and pacifists in America would appreciate Japan's character. They would wish to cooperate with Japan and repress the imperialists." The Fleet faction was counting on the strong antiwar movement in America to advance its selfish cause. In this struggle Admiral Heihachiro Togo emerged from retirement to come down flatly on the side of the Fleet faction, which was advocating unlimited construction of heavy cruisers. In fact Togo became the strongest advocate of the Fleet faction and his support began to influence younger officers.

"We have already yielded thirty percent," said Togo. "If they do not concede to us on this very important matter of the heavy cruisers, we can only give the conference up as hopeless and return home. Even if we are defeated, there will be no naval expansion. Therefore there is nothing to worry about fiscally. We have adopted the position that without seventy percent we cannot feel secure in our national defense. Consequently petty bargaining over one or two percentage points is useless. If they will not accommodate our demands, the only thing to do is resolutely to withdraw from the conference."

But Prime Minister Hamaguchi was determined that the London Naval Conference should not fail through Japan's obstinacy, and Prince Saionji, the emperor's principal advisor, felt the same. So did the emperor. As a very junior member of the delegation, Yamamoto's views were not considered, but he took his cue from Admiral Hori, with whom he had been discussing Japan's naval strengths and needs for ten years.

While the discussions within the navy were in progress, Admiral Suetsugu without authority held a press conference and issued a statement that Japan could accept no compromise. This threw Japanese politics and the conference into a tailspin.

The Fleet faction of the Navy campaigned vigorously against the treaty and aroused a large segment of the public to believe that the treaty would seriously threaten Japan's defense capability. The National League of Students Opposed to the Traitorous Treaty (a right-wing group) issued a statement charging the government with knuckling under to American demands, and throwing Japanese defenses away and endangering the foundation of military command. The group called for the resignation of the cabinet and the junking of the treaty. This view was prevalent on the ultraright or nationalist level and created a constant stir against the treaty.

The Fleet faction continued the demand that the Japanese in London ask for parity, which meant a 5-5-5 ship ratio, and the Japanese delegation did ask, but their hearts were not in it. Yamamoto was quite content with the sixty plus percent ratio, as were the principal delegates. Since they could not hope to defeat the Americans in war, Yamamoto argued, what was the need for parity? Admiral Kanji Kato and Admiral Nobemasu Suetsugu were adamant, and when the Japanese delegation failed to secure the parity they demanded, Admiral Kato resigned from the navy in anger and began a campaign to win control of the navy for the Fleet faction.

When the delegation returned to Tokyo in the spring of 1930 the Fleet faction urged rejection of the treaty. In the end the treaty was saved by the personal intervention of Emperor Hirohito, but the breach created in the Imperial Navy was irreparable.

During the conference the expansion-minded army had been creating trouble in China. A large segment of the public, egged on by the newspapers, had become expansionist. To them the treaty meant the end of their hopes for a powerful navy. Admiral Kanji Kato kept the fires of dissent burning. Admiral Yamamoto spoke out in favor of the treaty, and thus became well known as an advocate of peace, and a target of the right wing. So heated was the argument that in the midst of it a young activist tried to assassinate Prime Minister Hamaguchi and wounded him seriously.

It was the beginnning of an era that a foreign reporter aptly named "government by assassination." Many liberal political leaders suddenly disappeared from the scene, in fear of assassination. Many others became silent on matters of international import and Japanese expansion. The army, backed by the Fleet faction of the navy, was preparing to destroy the political parties and impose military rule.

Following the return of the treaty delegation, Admiral Yamamoto welcomed an appointment that removed him from the political sphere. He was appointed director of the navy's Aeronautics Department and took over the responsibility for building the infant air force. His efforts produced the Zero fighter, the Nakajima torpedo attack plane and the twin engined bomber known to Americans later as the Betty. By 1933 work was beginning on these new aircraft that would be the best in the world in the late 1930s. The tragedy on the *Akagi* caused him to order systems of homing and carrier operation devised to improve safety. He also saw that the limitation of armaments would prevent the naval aviation arm from expanding quickly, so he developed the idea of the air fleet, an independent air force that could quickly be converted for carrier use but was equally suited to operate from land bases against naval targets. It was a concept ten years ahead of the West.

By 1931 the Japanese navy had fourteen new squadrons of wheeled aircraft in service in these fleets and a total air capability unmatched in quality and quantity by the Western world. In 1933 Yamamoto's term as director of aeronautics expired, and he went back to sea as commander of the First Air Division of the navy. The idea of an air division, too, was a new concept. The Japanese felt that the massing of carriers created a powerful force, and so they adopted what the Americans would later copy as a multiple carrier task force. Yamamoto had the concept and Yamamoto carried it out. Whereas the Western powers still considered the battleship fleets the primary naval striking force, Yamamoto proposed to use as many as six carriers operating together, as the attack force. As commander he brought strict discipline to the naval air force and established a tradition that would last through the Second World War.

The Japanese army began its bid for political power with the seizure of Manchuria in 1931, followed by an attempt to seize Shanghai and seizure of more areas of North China and the establishment of a large military garrison in Tientsin. Yamamoto was lucky to be where he was. His friend Admiral Hori was dragooned to lead a naval expedition against Shanghai in 1932, and was roundly criticized because he refused to fire on civilians. Such was the gathering storm of war fever in Japan that almost any warlike act was greeted by the public with enthusiasm. The military adventuring had begun.

As a loyal Japanese officer, Yamamoto said nothing of his views of what was happening in China and what threatened to happen elsewhere in the world. He was definitely of two minds about Japan's future. First, he relished the idea of Japan becoming an equal with the Western powers. He shared a general view among intelligent Japanese leaders that Japan should lead all Asia out of colonialism. Others stated the idea bluntly: it was high time for the white man to be evicted from control of Asian affairs. But tempering that view was his conviction that Japan should never engage in war with the West because Japan would lose such a war.

Therefore he wanted to play a game of waiting, building Japan's industrial and military strength, but not flexing her muscles the way Germany was doing.

But further events were occurring in Tokyo that threw control of the Navy into the hands of the Fleet faction.

By 1934 the Fleet faction of the Navy had secured important posts in the planning section of the Imperial Navy staff and the Navy Ministry. Admiral Kanji Kato had come back to service, and he and Admiral Suetsugu overpowered the Treaty faction admirals. Their instrument had been Admiral Mineo Osumi, who became Minister of the Navy in January 1933. He was not a member of the Fleet faction but he was a weak man and was soon controlled by these men of strong personality who used him to destroy their enemies. They demanded and secured the retirement of prominent members of the Treaty faction who had controlled naval policy in the past. They went after Admiral Takeichi Hori, Yamamoto's classmate and best friend, accusing him of cowardice when he was in command of the Japanese squadron in Shanghai during the incident of 1932. The charge stemmed from the fact that he had been asked by the army to open fire on Chinese troops in the factory area and had delayed because too many civilians were in the area. So Hori's sense of humanity was now used against him.

The Fleet faction waited impatiently for the naval treaties of 1922 and 1930 to expire. In fact they did not really wait. They laid plans and drew blueprints for four superbattleships of 72,000 tons each, which would mount eighteen-inch guns, the largest in the world. They made blueprints for new destroyers and cruisers. Since most of them were battleship men they paid no attention to the aeronautical needs of the Navy. (This, in fact, was the source of Yamamoto's strength and the reason they had not gone after him. In spite of his views, the Fleet faction respected Yamamoto for his technical abilities and knowledge and knew they needed him. He had obliged so far by ignoring politics, having stated his views on war and peace.)

In the spring of 1934, Kato's Fleet faction of the navy and the army joined forces in their first move for military control of the government. The first overt act was to deny members of the Diet information about the army and navy budgets, which came to forty-three percent of the total budget of the government. When Diet members demanded details, Minister of War Araki said they were military secrets and Minister Osumi backed him up. The Diet did not get the figures. The militarists had won the first round in their battle for control of the national government.

Thus when Yamamoto was suddenly appointed chief delegate to the London Naval conference of 1934 at the request of the Emperor, the Fleet faction did not try to block his appointment. They only demanded that he and the delegation hold out for parity with the Western powers in this new series of meetings.

So Yamamoto went to London, where he was affable and open, but where he faced men who no longer trusted Japan. The military adventures in Manchuria and China had soured the Westerners, and they were unwilling to even consider any program that would add to Japan's power of aggression. In a series of face-to-face meetings with the British and the Americans, Yamamoto got absolutely nowhere, and five days before Christmas 1934, the Americans suddenly decided the conference was a waste of time and packed up and went home to Washington.

The conference resumed later but made no progress.

There was nothing for the Japanese delegation to do but come home. They stopped in Berlin and then took the Trans-Siberian railroad east. In Berlin Yamamoto was asked if he wanted to meet Adolf Hitler. Foreign Minister Yosuke Matsuoka was negotiating with the Germans and the Italians to

Admiral Yamamoto is greeted by an honor guard on his return to Tokyo from the London Naval Conference (Feb. 12, 1935).
(Bottom) Admiral Yamamoto (second from left) discussing the conference with Cabinet members.

join the Rome-Berlin alliance. Yamamoto, who detested the idea, refused to meet Hitler and went on home.

Back in Tokyo he visited the Navy Ministry and announced the failure of the conference. Minister Osumi and other other leaders of the "new" navy were delighted. It was only a matter of weeks until the 1922 treaty expired, and they jumped the gun and began the construction of the superbattleships immediately. The die was cast for a runaway building program destined to make the Imperial Navy the strongest in the Pacific by 1941.

Admiral Yamamoto now posed a problem for the new men of the navy. They knew he was admired by the Emperor and they were afraid of him. They decided that even if he was the navy's foremost aviation leader they would push him into retirement and very nearly did. They gave him a big office in the Navy Ministry and nothing to do. For months he sat and twiddled his fingers, or traveled around the country. He spent much time in the geisha houses. He talked about quitting the navy and moving to Monte Carlo to become a professional gambler. He was so quiet that the Fleet faction leaders began to think he was under their control, and they respected his technical achievements so much that they decided to employ him as chief of the naval air forces. It was an ideal appointment for Yamamoto, who had all the abilities and knowledge to carry it out. He spent the rest of the year 1935, then, in finishing the job he had begun four years earlier as technical chief of the air force, building a thoroughly modern naval air force that would lead those of all other nations. This task involved refining the new naval fighting aircraft, establishing new air fleets and squadrons, developing new techniques of search and recovery, and utilizing a whole gamut of skills. He developed the Kawanishi flying boat, which became the finest long range-search plane in World War II, giving the Japanese an immense advantage over the Americans in fleet intelligence. It was a happy year for Yamamoto after all, and at the end of it he had succeeded beyond his dreams. The nation's shipbuilders were persuaded to cooperate in the rebuilding of old carriers and the construction of new. Under Yamamoto's influence, one of the new battleship hulls was converted to become a giant carrier and before his term ended the super carrier *Shinano* was nearly ready to begin construction. Japan would soon have ten aircraft carriers, more than any other nation, more than the six that the United States had in service.

3

Yamamoto and the Militarists

At the end of 1935, as his happy year drew to a close, Admiral Yamamoto knew that he had made of the Japanese fleet the most powerful naval air force in the world. There was no need for Japan to fear attack from anyone. But Yamamoto observed the political scene with a growing sense of isolation and despair. He saw the militarists gain power every day and he seriously considered resigning his commission or retiring. Then, in the early months of 1936, the militarists overplayed their hand.

On February 26, four regiments of the Army were persuaded by leaders of the Action faction to rebel and try to seize power. They took over many of the government offices, tried to assassinate the prime minister and did kill or wound many of the high officials of government. But the revolution failed because Emperor Hirohito stepped in, for the first time in his reign. He told the senior generals that they would bring the rebellious troops under control or he would personally lead the Imperial Guard out to fight in the streets of Tokyo. Alarmed, the generals tried to temporize but Hirohito would not listen to them. The generals then acted, and after four days the crisis ended in the surrender of the rebels, the suicide of some ringleaders, and the trial and execution of others. Many generals were retired. The Control faction emerged in undisputed control of the army but this rebellion had been a warning from the junior officers, who had become increasingly unruly, and the Control faction and Action faction merged and began their effort to force a military oligarchy on the country.

They moved more cautiously, and Japan enjoyed a brief respite from military agitation. In revulsion against the army, Emperor Hirohito went outside the usual corridors of power and chose a commoner civilian, Koki Hirota, to be the new prime minister in the hope that he would preserve civil government. Admiral Mitsumasa Yonai, the leader of the moderates in the navy, was selected to be navy minister. He chose Yamamoto as his vice minister.

Yamamoto did not want this political job and said so, but Yonai persuaded him to accept in the interest of keeping the navy out of the hands of the Fleet faction.

The army lay quiet and made no objection to the appointments. But the generals did make one request of the new prime minister to prevent any new schisms within the service. In the future the minister of the army should be selected only from officers on active duty. Hirota saw nothing amiss in this request and honored it. Quietly the Supreme War Council, which was dominated by the militarist generals and admirals, secured passage of a constitutional amendment that made the new rule part of the basic law of Japan.

Early in 1937 the Hirota government fell over Hirota's attempts to conciliate China in the face of violent army opposition. The army minister resigned and the army cabal refused to appoint another for the Hirota cabinet. Under the Constitution the cabinet was required to have both a war minister and a navy minister. Even then the army was quiescent but suggested the name of General Senjuro Hayashi as premier designate. Hayashi was known as a moderate and Hirohito thought he could control the army, and so appointed Hayashi, who retained Admirals Yonai and Yamamoto in their posts. But in May 1937 the army demanded a more militant national policy and when Hayashi failed to impose it, they withdrew the army minister and the Hayashi cabinet collapsed.

When the Hayashi government fell the army expected to get one of the oligarchy—General Hajime Sugiyama—into power, but Hirohito did not trust Sugiyama and he appointed Prince Fumimaro Konoye on the condition that he would keep Yonai and Yamamoto as a balance to the army. Konoye complied but he allowed himself to be persuaded to appoint General Sadao Araki, one of the most powerful and militant officers, as education minister, which threw the whole Japanese educational system into the hands of the army. The new education minister immediately began to promulgate emperor worship—in spite of the objections of Hirohito. The army also forced the appointment of General Sugiyama as army minister. The stage was being set by the army to take control of all Japan.

In June 1937 General Hideki Tojo, commander of the Kwantung army, reported that China was arranging a treaty with Outer Mongolia aimed at preventing further Japanese inroads into North China and he advocated a preemptive strike against China. The generals in Tokyo agreed. Thus was set the stage for the incident at the Marco Polo Bridge when Chinese and Japanese troops clashed, and the beginning of the new war with China. The army was united behind this war policy and there was absolutely nothing that Yonai and Yamamoto could do to stop it.

Admiral Yonai and Admiral Yamamoto tried to prevent the poison from spreading, but every time other cabinet ministers objected to army policies, the army threatened to withdraw General Sugiyama as war minister and so force the collapse of the cabinet. So by the fall of 1937 army control of the Japanese government was complete. With the introduction of food rationing and increased conscription, the whole country was placed on a war footing.

At the end of the Russo-Japanese War, Admiral Togo could say proudly to his Russian counterparts "we are not barbarians," but by the end of 1937 that had changed. The murder of 250,000 Chinese men, women, and children, soldiers and civilians, in the Rape of Nanking, convinced the world that the Japanese army's behavior was barbaric in the extreme.

At the time of the Nanking massacre the navy became directly involved in the aggression in China. The Fleet faction was running the operations in China, and the officers in charge of the carriers encouraged the pilots to attack foreign shipping as well as Chinese. Thus one December day Japanese carrier planes attacked and sank the American gunboat *Panay* on the Yangtze River.

This was a very serious offense against international law and could have brought a war that even Japan was not yet ready to contemplate. U.S. Ambassador Joseph Grew prepared to leave Tokyo, certain that his government would break off diplomatic relations. When Admiral Yamamoto learned what had happened he rushed to the American embassy, apologized profusely, called the attack a "dreadful mistake" and offered indemnity. Of course it was not a mistake at all, but planned provocation by the Fleet faction. Yamamoto's obvious sincerity convinced Ambassador Grew that the Japanese government regretted the incident and would prevent future incidents.

When Admiral Mitsunami, the man who had authorized the attack, came back to Tokyo, Admiral Yonai castigated him publicly in a way seldom done in Japan, and fired him on the spot.

Admiral Yamamoto issued a public statement in English and Japanese:

"The Imperial Navy, which bore responsibility for this

incident, takes this opportunity to express its gratification at the fairness and perspicacity shown, despite a barrage of misunderstanding and propaganda, by the American public in appreciating the true facts of the incident and Japan's good faith in dealing with it. It also expresses the deep gratitude for the dispassionate and understanding attitude adopted by the Japanese public since the occurrence of the incident.

"The navy will, of course, take redoubled precautions to ensure the eradication of incidents of this type, but at the same time it earnestly hopes that the entire nation will help turn misfortune to good advantage by cooperating in the furthering of international understanding and friendship via the removal of misapprehensions and suspicions that come between Japan and other nations concerned in the 'China Incident'."

The statement was not solely for foreign consumption; it was also a warning in plain Japanese that the hawks of the Fleet faction had very nearly brought Japan into a war she was not ready to fight. The navy militants were cowed temporarily.

As 1938 began, the relative quiet that followed the *Panay* Incident began to dissolve. The Fleet faction stirred its younger members up to threaten Admiral Yonai and Admiral Inouye, his assistant, and Vice Minister Yamamoto. All three received death threats. Yamamoto showed great aplomb in this period. One night as he was going to the British embassy he had to move through a crowd outside who threatened him. His worst worry came when the Army insisted on assigning members of the *kempeitai* military police to "protect" him. He was certain that at some point, on some lonely street, they would make an attempt on his life. so he made sure that he was always accompanied by a couple of sailors.

The Yonai-Inouye-Yamamoto combine got through the

year 1938 without harm. Early in January 1939 the Konoye cabinet collapsed over the army insistence that the government join the Berlin-Rome alliance. This alliance, as Foreign Minister Matsuoka admitted,was aimed at Washington. A new cabinet was formed by Kiichiro Hiranuma. Again, at the Emperor's request, Admiral Yonai and Admiral Yamamoto were retained but it was apparent that their struggles were in vain and the army was gaining power every week.

The Hiranuma cabinet's short life was dominated by the issue of the Rome-Berlin-Tokyo alliance, which Yonai and Yamamoto opposed. This issue caused the collapse of the Hiranuma cabinet in August 1939 when Hitler shocked the world by making an alliance with Russia.

General Abe was chosen to be the new Prime Minister and he wanted a docile navy minister, so Yonai and Yamamoto were out. One of Admiral Yonai's last acts as navy minister was to send Admiral Yamamoto to sea as commander of the Combined Fleet to get him out of Tokyo and save his life. Yamamoto went gratefully. There was nothing more that he could do to avoid the steady march of Japan toward war.

So on August 20, 1939, Admiral Yamamoto went to the Imperial Palace for investiture as commander of the Combined Fleet. He had made that fleet's naval air force into the most powerful in the world. Now he would be forced to prepare that navy for a war that he opposed.

4

Yamamoto and The Pacific War

In the fall of 1939 former Navy Minister Admiral Mitsumasa Yonai was persuaded to form a government. He was the last hope of the Emperor that the Army takeover of civil government could be resisted. But actually there was no hope. The Army was determined to have its way. The issue was the signing of the treaty that bound Japan to Germany and Italy. The argument over that issue caused the Yonai government to collapse in July 1940.

By that time Admiral Yamamoto was well along in installing new discipline and a new sense of well-being in the Combined Fleet. He concentrated on gunnery training, night maneuvers and ship handling, and had his captains so confident that they welcomed the night training exercises.

Prince Konoye came back to govern, and his new policy of disbanding the political parties and establishing a unified government was put into effect. What it really meant was that the army was in control and, as Admiral Yamamoto realized, war with the West was inevitable. As a patriotic Japanese citizen, he prepared to fight that war although he had no confidence in victory. As he told Prince Konoye one day that fall, "I can run wild for the first six months, but after that...." And he spoke meaningfully of America's enormous industrial capacity.

The only course that Yamamoto could see for Japan was to start strong, win those early victories, and by disabling the American fleet at the beginning of the war, perhaps achieve a situation in which the Americans and the British could be brought to the peace table to accept Japan's conquests. Perhaps. He gave it not even a fifty-fifty chance of success.

The key to any chance at all was the crippling of the American Pacific Fleet at the outset of the war, and the only way to be sure of doing this was to launch a preemptive strike just as Admiral Togo had done in 1904 against the Russian Pacific Squadron at Port Arthur.

The army was not much interested in this aspect of the coming war. The generals could see no further than their noses. They needed rubber, tin, and oil and they could get it in Malaya and the Dutch East Indies. The only question the army asked was whether they should strike north, and get the resources from Siberia, or south. After two abortive attempts to test the possibilities of striking Russia, both of them disastrous to Japan, they decided to strike south.

In September 1940 the Japanese moved into northern Indo-China. This action precipitated the first major crisis with the Americans, who cut off Japan's shipments of scrap iron and steel. In Tokyo this American action made war almost inevitable. The first step, as far as the navy was concerned, was the calling of a conference in Tokyo to get approval of the admirals for the pact with Germany and Italy. Admiral Yamamoto went up from his flagship for the meeting, armed with arguments against the treaty, saw when he got there that the cabinet members' minds were made up, and abruptly quit arguing. He went back to the flagship and began preparations to load the Indo-China airfields with navy planes from the new air fleets. The decision to move into northern Indo-China was presented as a matter of facilitating attacks on Chinese airfields, but it was, in fact, the first preparation for the assault on Malaya.

The role of Admiral Yamamoto and the Imperial Navy was to move and protect the troops as they conquered Malaya and the Dutch East Indies. The Philippines assault was an afterthought, thrown in to deprive the United States of a base in the Western Pacific. But a strike against the American fleet was not in the Army plan. In 1940 the army and navy high commands opposed it. But Admiral Yamamoto considered all the possibilities. He kept coming back to the American fleet. This fleet could be a final obstacle. In his mind that obstacle had to be eliminated first of all.

To test this idea he approached one man whose judgment on matters of air power he respected, Vice Admiral Takejiro Ohnishi, an airman who had served under his command several times since graduation from the naval academy at Eta Jima. Ohnishi was at first aghast at the idea of sending a striking force halfway across the Pacific to get at the American Pacific fleet in Pearl Harbor. Yamamoto proposed to use several carriers and this was also unheard of in fleet doctrine. Carriers operated in single units, as part of battle forces. Why, said Admiral Ohnishi, they might lose half a dozen ships in such a wild adventure!

Yes, replied Admiral Yamamoto, but what was the alternative? He expounded on America's productive capacities, as he had observed them years before. The Americans at this point had only half a dozen carriers, split between the Pacific and the Atlantic fleets, and no new ones. But if war came the Americans would soon be building carriers, and in a few months they might have a dozen. If Japan was to win a struggle with America it must be done at the outset, and so demoralize the Americans by defeat that they would come to the peace table and accept Japan's ambitions for leadership in Asia. That was the only way that Yamamoto could see to avoid ultimate ignominious defeat.

One by one Yamamoto overcame Ohnishi's objections,

and the younger admiral became convinced, and then became the principal supporter of the Yamamoto plan. He drew up a report that outlined the program, and Yamamoto then sent him to Tokyo to begin the arduous task of convincing the naval establishment that this must be the new fleet doctrine. The Combined Fleet would be recast around a carrier striking force rather then the present battleship force. The air war would be the war of the future.

Ohnishi's mission to Tokyo was not very successful; only when Yamamoto said the attack on the American Pacific fleet was absolutely necessary and he would resign as commander of the fleet if it was not acceptable did the Japanese military establishment begin to listen, but they still did not accept the plan. Yet, even as the Pearl Harbor attack plan was being made in detail, Admiral Yamamoto was doing what he could to persuade others that the whole military adventure was doomed to disaster.

On July 2, 1941, the decision was made in Tokyo to invade southern Indo-China to prepare bases for assault on Malaya. The U.S. responded by cutting off all oil supplies to Japan. Yamamoto was summoned to Tokyo to be informed of the decision. When he heard Navy Minister Nagano's report, he shrugged his shoulders as though he did not care.

"There's nothing we can do now," he said. And he went back to his flagship to prepare for the war with America. One of his first acts was to organize the new air fleets to take over the southern Indo-China air bases.

In August of 1941, Admiral Yamamoto sent the carrier *Akagi* to Kagoshima on the southern tip of Kyushu island for training exercises. This was to be special training for an air attack against ships anchored in the harbor. Someone had noticed that the harbor at Kagoshima bore a striking resemblance to Pearl Harbor, from the mountain background to the layout of the anchorages. Kagoshima was slated to be the principal training ground for the Pearl Harbor air attack.

Admiral Yamamoto chose Lieutenant Commander Mitsuo Fuchida to lead the air strike on the American warships, and Fuchida took over the training program. Soon other carriers of the First Air Fleet arrived at Kagoshima. Immediately a problem was presented. The Japanese aerial torpedoes would not function in such confined waters. They needed open space for their warheads to arm after they struck the water.

"Fix it," said Admiral Yamamoto.

So the torpedo experts started to adjust the torpedoes to function in confined waters. At the same time the dive bombers and level bombers started their practicing on targets in and around Kagoshima.

By midsummer 1941 Admiral Yamamoto's plan for the attack on Pearl Harbor still had not been accepted by the naval high command. Among those who opposed it was Vice Admiral Chuichi Nagumo. When Yamamoto learned of the reception he sent his chief of staff, Vice Admiral Matome Ugaki, to emphasize to the naval high command that if they did not undertake the Pearl Harbor attack, Yamamoto would quit as commander of the Combined Fleet. Ultimately the high command yielded to the reorganization of fleet resources demanded. But Yamamoto was upset to learn that the personnel bureau chose Admiral Nagumo to lead the First Air Division in the assault. His chief of staff asked him if he wanted to demand a change of commanders. Yamamoto said such an action would demoralize the attack force and he would stick with Nagumo, who, however, would have to be carefully instructed as to his responsibilities.

On October 31, 1941, Yamamoto was suddenly summoned to Tokyo by Admiral Shigetaro Shimada, the navy minister. Sensing that there was still some doubt about the certainty of war, Admiral Yamamoto took with him statistics to argue against war. He intended to bring out all the details of Japan's shortage of materials, facts of which he had been well aware since the days as technical director of the navy air force, when he had been given the responsibility to develop new weapons.

But when Yamamoto got to Tokyo he learned that the senior officers of the navy had been called together only to put the imprimatur of the navy on the war. Prime Minister Konoye had resigned. General Hideki Tojo had become prime minister. The new navy minister was Tojo's stooge. Shimada stated the purpose of the meeting, and then asked if anyone had any questions. Admiral Yamamoto asked one question. How much of a petroleum reserve did Japan have at the moment? The minister responded that this did not make any difference, because Japan would assure her petroleum supply by taking the Dutch East Indies oil fields. With that, Yamamoto knew that the last hope for peace had vanished, and he made no further statements. The minister announced that all the admirals were in favor of the war.

On November 17, Admiral Yamamoto held a going-away party for Admiral Nagumo and the senior officers of the Pearl Harbor striking force, at which he made one last stab at peace. "Should the negotiations with the United States now in progress in Washington be successful," he said, "we shall order our forces to withdraw. If such an order is received, you are to turn about and come back to base, even if the attack force has already taken off from the carriers."

After the order was once given it would be too late, said Admiral Nagumo.

Admiral Yamamoto glared at him. "If there is any commander here who doesn't think he could come back if he got the order, I forbid him to go. He can hand in his resignation now."

He was greeted by silence.

Next morning the striking force sailed for Hitokappu Bay in the Kurils, north of Honshu island. This was the secret assembly point for the striking force. They came silently till

Planes take off from the deck of the aircraft carrier *Akagi*, as the Pearl Harbor attack begins.

all had arrived, six carriers, two battleships to protect them and enough cruisers and destroyers for all the tasks that were to be done. Separately more than twenty submarines were moving in to scout the route and help with the attack.

On the morning of November 26 the striking force sailed from the Kurils.

On the afternoon of December 1 a final conference was held at the Imperial Palace and General Tojo outlined the plans for the beginning of the war. He asked for comments. There were none. He adjourned the meeting.

The next day Admiral Yamamoto came up from the fleet base at Hachirajima near Kure. From Naval Headquarters he sent off the prearranged signal: "Climb Mount Niitaka," which was the code to launch the attack.

The next morning he went to the Navy Ministry for a ceremonial party honoring the mission, and then he met his friend former Admiral Hori, who had been forced out of the navy by the fleet faction and was now a shipbuilder.

"Look after yourself" said Hori as they parted.

"Thanks," said Yamamoto. "I don't imagine I'll be back...."

Now all that could stop the Pearl Harbor attack was a callback order that would mean the Japanese and Americans had reached agreement in Washington. There was no callback. Just before dawn on December 7 (Hawaii time), 183 aircraft of the first Pearl Harbor attack wave took off from the six carriers and headed 150 miles to Hawaii on their mission of destruction. Within four hours the American battleship fleet was in shambles. But what about the American carriers, which to Yamamoto were the most important? They had been out on training missions and they were all missed, even one carrier that the Japanese knew was in the immediate vicinity because they shot down some of its planes. The fleet air staff pleaded with Admiral Nagumo to make a second strike on the submarine and oil facilities, which would incapacitate the Pearl Harbor base for months, and wait for the carriers. But Admiral Nagumo was too nervous. He had accomplished the letter, if not the spirit, of his instructions and he had not lost any ships. That was enough for him, and he refused to authorize any more air strikes or to wait around for the return of the carriers.

When Admiral Yamamoto's chief of staff learned that Nagumo had left Pearl Harbor without finishing the job, he wanted Yamamoto to order the striking force to return to the scene, but it was the privilege of the commander to make such decisions, Yamamoto said. He would not interfere although he was sorely disappointed at the failure. The chief of staff persuaded him to order an attack on Midway on the way home, but Nagumo did not even do that, pleading bad weather.

The Pearl Harbor attack was announced in Tokyo as a perfect success. The American battleship fleet had been crippled. The high command expected Yamamoto to be happy. But Yamamoto knew that the strike on Pearl Harbor had failed to cripple the American fleet's power to strike back. Those battleships that had been disabled were all outmoded, and the Americans were already building new ones. Yamamoto knew that it would all have to be done over.

But as he had predicted, the war began with one Japanese victory after another. The carrier striking force was sent to the South Pacific in February to support the invasion of the Dutch East Indies, and raided Darwin, Australia, frightening the whole continent, but achieving very little militarily. Nagumo was sent into the Indian Ocean in April, where he attacked the British naval base at Trincomalee and Colombo, sinking two cruisers and the old carrier *Hermes*, but missing the two new carriers of the British East Asia Fleet.

The Japanese propaganda machine began to sound the note that Japan was invincible, and soon enough many generals and admirals began to believe it. Yamamoto never did. He wanted to take the second step, which was to lure the American fleet out to fight and then destroy the carriers. To do this Yamamoto insisted on the Midway invasion in June.

The Navy ministry did not like the Midway attack. It put the whole Combined Fleet at risk. Who ever heard of employing eight carriers in one operation? And that is precisely what Yamamoto was insisting on, six fleet carriers against Midway, with one light carrier in reserve, and one carrier against the Aleutians. But again Yamamoto offered to quit and in the end again he had his way.

The Battle of the Coral Sea threw a monkey wrench into Yamamoto's plans. The carriers *Shokaku* and *Zuikaku*, involved in the action, both suffered damage; one was temporarily disabled and the other lost most of its aircraft and pilots. The repairs and the replacements took time and so these two carriers were not available for the Midway operation.

At Midway, once again Yamamoto's plan was undone by Admiral Nagumo. Part of the problem was that the American navy had broken the Japanese naval code and thus the element of surprise was lost to the Japanese. But this was not the reason for the defeat and loss of all Japanese fleet carriers at Midway. The defeat was caused by Admiral Nagumo's failure to send search planes out early enough and far enough in the Midway operation to find the American fleet waiting in ambush. He had no suspicion that the Americans had been alerted and had arrived off Midway when the Japanese believed them still to be tucked safely in Pearl Harbor.

After Midway, Japan still had the edge in carriers that June of 1942, but it was sharply reduced and the American shipbuilding program promised that the Japanese edge would be eliminated in a few months.

Now the war settled down to a slogging match, in which Admiral Yamamoto knew Japan must ultimately be defeated.

His one hope was to come to grips with the American fleet before the enemy had time to build it up. When the Americans invaded Guadalcanal, Yamamoto moved fleet

Yamamoto salutes pilots about to fly a mission out of Rabaul in the South Pacific.

headquarters to Truk in the South Pacific, so he could get to grips with the Americans. Once again Admiral Nagumo failed him in several inconclusive encounters with the American carriers. Yamamoto watched as the Americans built their fleet, and after he lost the battleships *Hiei* and *Kirishima* in a single action, he sensed that the war had turned around.

Guadalcanal was lost because of the staying power of the American marines in the early days, while the Americans fought to secure air control of the area. Yamamoto was hard pressed to try to supply the troops on Guadalcanal, and in the late autumn of 1942, the army missed its chances to secure a land victory. American air power had become so strong that resupply became impossible. Yamamoto then conducted a brilliant withdrawal from the island, but withdrawals do not win wars.

Considering the next step in the South and Southwest Pacific and the army's insistence on continuing its operations against New Guinea, Yamamoto tried to wipe out American air power in the Southwest Pacific and South Pacific commands. In March he planned a major week-long air operation. He was completely misled by the pilots and air crews, who came back from their missions with enormously exaggerated claims of success. If Yamamoto did not believe them, at least he pretended to do so, and Tokyo announced the program as an enormous victory, when in fact it was not.

Early on Yamamoto had told his friend Hori that he sensed that he would not see the end of the war. In the spring of 1943, having just carried out that extended air attack against Guadalcanal and New Guinea, Admiral Yamamoto decided on a risky flight to visit the front-line air bases to encourage his naval air forces to greater effort. The Americans, intercepting a secret coded message about Yamamoto's itinerary, ambushed his plane over Bougainville, and he was killed when the plane was shot down. Thus perished the man the Americans considered to be their primary naval opponent. And thus, also, perished his genius for improvising plans. Japan had begun the war with the strongest naval weapons, the Zero fighter, dive bombers and torpedo bombers that were superior to those of the Western navies, the best torpedoes, and the best ability for destroyer fighting and for night fighting. Gradually these advantages were lost as the Americans developed the the Grumman F6F fighter, which was engineered specifically to counter the Zero, and the TBF torpedo bomber. The Americans improved their torpedoes, and the edge of Japanese night fighting ability was blunted by American radar, which more than evened the odds. The technological superiority that Yamamoto had given the Japanese navy was lost and ultimately so was the war.

Had he lived, the Japanese naval war effort would have been pursued far more vigorously that it was after April 1943. Yamamoto knew the deficiencies of his aircraft and the improved version of the Zero fighter, which was a far closer match for the Grumman F6F, would have been rushed into production. Also, his staff had made a plan for a carrier attack on the Panama Canal. After his death, however, Japan's naval stance became defensive. Yamamoto was the only Japanese naval commander who had any cogent plans for the prosecution of the war.

Beyond that, he would not have feared to press for surrender after the loss of Saipan in July 1944, and he would have been the logical successor to General Tojo as a prime minister who could extricate Japan from the war.

As it is, Admiral Yamamoto left a great military legacy to Japan. His strategic concept of the war was followed after his death until the sea battle of the Marianas, after which the Combined Fleet was so diminished that its name was dropped and the fleet was called the Mobile Force. At the battle of Leyte Gulf it was almost completely destroyed.

Yamamoto's contention that Japan needed only a naval force capable of self-defense was adopted after World War

II with the creation of the Self-Defense Forces. His understanding of the naval air arm's power persists in the Naval
Self-Defense Force but practically that aspect of naval
defense in the 1990s was still in American hands. Yamamoto's deep feeling that Japan should get along with her neighbors has become Self-Defense Force policy.

Tactically and technologically most of Yamamoto's con-
tributions have been surpassed by weapons development and
time. But some of them persist. Yamamoto believed in strict
discipline at sea and maximum effort in making the best use
of the weapons and facilities at hand. His Combined Fleet
had the best sea discipline of any naval fighting force in the
world, and was particularly competent in night fighting at
every level, not just destroyers. Those legacies have been
retained. American officers who have served aboard Japanese naval vessels in the postwar years have been emphatic in
their praise of the sea discipline of the Naval Self-Defense
Force, and the proof of the efficiency has been the low acci-
dent rate. After Yamamoto's death, some of his memorabilia
were enshrined at the museum of the Eta Jima Naval Academy near Hiroshima, along with those of Admiral Lord Nel-
son and Admiral Togo. He is in fitting company.

PART
III

Tomoyuki Yamashita

General Tomoyuki Yamashita.

1

Tomoyuki Yamashita and
the Army Militarists

Tomoyuki Yamashita was born on November 8, 1885, in a small village on the island of Shikoku. His father was the local doctor, and so as a boy he had every advantage that the village could offer. He grew up strong and muscular, but never showed much interest in reading and writing and he stood very low in his school class. His family had hoped that he might become a doctor, but soon saw that he was not cut out for an academic or medical career, although they still hoped that he would achieve something from education.

When he was twelve years old he was sent to the provincial capital, twenty-five miles away from the village, and enrolled in the Kainan Middle School, This old school, with a proud tradition, was founded by the local daimyo in the days of the shogunate to educate samurai. Nearly twenty years before Tomoyuki was born Japan had been rudely yanked out of feudalism. The samurai had disappeared and so had the shogunate. They had been replaced by the Meiji constitutional monarchy, and the process of building a modern army and navy had begun. But Kainan Middle School—the School of the Southern Sea—had adjusted to the changes and become an academy for the training of boys who would join the army and aspire to become officers. The training of the young boys had not changed much. They wore a samurai-style uniform, kimono with a sort of kilt underneath. They learned to march and to imitate fighting by practicing *kendo*, with wooden sword and protective mask. They marched in heavy boots carrying a heavy knapsack. Each boy had a rifle, which he learned to shoot and kept always at his side. After two years at the Kainan Middle School, Tomoyuki decided that he wanted to be a soldier and he came home to announce his decision to his mother.

The Imperial Army offered a true profession to young Japanese. They could rise through the ranks to rub shoulders with the elite of the country. In this sense the army was one of the most democratic institutions in Japan. Yamashita's father could see that the boy was not cut out for intellectual life and agreed that he should become a soldier. In 1900 Tomoyuki went off to the cadet academy at Hiroshima, one of the schools established by the Meiji government for the training of young soldiers.

It was the year of the Boxer Rebellion, and soldiers of Japan for the first time found themselves on an equal footing with those of the Western powers which had so lately tried to colonize Japan as they had China and other Asian countries. The Japanese army had provided a brigade to quell the Boxer uprising and Japanese troops had marched from Tientsin to Peking and occupied the Chinese capital. They had behaved impeccably and their bravery in the fighting had established a fine reputation for the new Japanese army. This development was all a result of the prescience of the advisors to Emperor Meiji. Early on, after Commodore Perry had awakened the shogunate to the existence of a powerful world beyond their seas, the Japanese government had begun the lightning effort already noted at modernization and industrialization and it had so far succeeded by 1900 that Japan was truly a power in the industrial and military senses.

The people of Japan were proud of their new status, and followed the Boxer Rebellion intently. One of the units involved was the Eleventh Imperial Army Regiment from Hiroshima. When the soldiers came back in their distinctive and colorful uniforms some of them were brought to the school to lecture and describe their experiences in China. They appeared in black jackets, the infantry with red trousers, the cavalry with green and the artillery with yellow, and all with smart French kepis on their heads. This splendor was enough to turn the head of any youth, and it reinforced Cadet Yamashita's yearning for the army life.

With the exception of such excitement, the routine at the academy was spartan in the extreme. The boys slept on wooden army cots and washed in cold water. They drilled every day, and also drilled into them were the army virtues of courage and fidelity, and unwavering obedience to orders, Reveille was at seven in the morning and the routine was carried out until nine p.m. when lights were turned out. Discipline was stern, and the qualities of the samurai were stressed in the training. There was no such thing as sport for sport's sake or leisure activity. Punishment for offenses was swift.

Under this harsh program Tomoyuki grew and prospered. He became one of the most skillful practitioners of *kendo*. And remarkably, this lacklustre student of the past also became something of a scholar, and rose to fourth in his class. After three years of cold-water discipline he was selected to go on for further military training. He left for Tokyo and the Central Military Academy that the Emperor Meiji had established. The Emperor took a personal interest in this school, and Yamashita saw him often, as the ruler attended all the school ceremonies and graduation exercises and often talked to the cadets. Once when the Diet was set to convene on the academy's graduation day, the Emperor postponed the meeting of the legislative body. On such occasions the cadets were invited to the Imperial Palace where they feasted on tea and cakes.

With the beginning of the Russo-Japanese war in 1904, the training of the cadets was stepped up, since the authorities thought they might be needed to replace the casualties of the war. They trained hard on the slopes of Mount Fuji, and they expected at any moment to be shipped to the front. But Yamashita's class was disappointed in the ending of the war before they had a chance for glory. Yamashita was commissioned a few months after the war ended, and posted to the Eleventh Regiment at Hiroshima. There he lived the life of a garrison soldier in peacetime, a dull life consisting of drill and routine.

Yamashita's ambition at that time was to secure an appointment to the General Staff College in Tokyo because therein lay the road to advancement and success in the military ranks. But appointment was achieved only by examination, and the examinations were very competitive. It took Lieutenant Yamashita several tries before he scored high enough to secure an appointment. In the interim, he served as a garrison officer. He distinguished himself with his attention to duty and imagination in planning and carrying out routine assignments and in training operations. His troops were well managed, well disciplined, and they performed well in maneuvers.

After several years he was promoted twice and was known as a "coming officer" among the junior officers of the time. As a captain he secured the appointment to the war college and went to Tokyo. During his last year at the war college he met the daughter of a general named Nagayama, and decided to ask her to marry him. He had turned down repeated proposals for arranged marriages to the daughters of businessmen and other officers, but he fell in love with Hisako Nagayama. Her father consented to a betrothal and they were married. Shortly afterward, in 1918, Yamashita was posted to the Japanese Embassy in Switzerland as assistant military attache and Hisako went to live with her parents while he went to Bern.

There he became friends with another Japanese army captain who was posted to the embassy. His name was Hideki Tojo. The two officers traveled around Germany, which had just been defeated in World War I, and practiced their German. By the end of his stay in Bern, Yamashita was proficient in that language, and after a stint back in Tokyo at Imperial Headquarters, he was sent abroad again, this time as military attache at Vienna. Again he went alone to Vienna, where he stayed for three years. While there he had an affair with the daughter of a German general, an association that strengthened his respect for Westerners.

When Yamashita returned to Japan in 1923 he was promoted to colonel and given command of the Third Regiment, one of the strongest in the Japanese army, which was headquartered in Tokyo. His fellow officer, Colonel Hideki Tojo, became deeply involved in the politics of the army. At this time the Action faction was threatening to take over the army and government and make sweeping changes.

In 1922 the Japanese economy went into a tailspin following the inflation after the world war. The silk market collapsed and many Japanese farm families were so near starvation that they sold their daughters into prostitution to survive. The young officers, having opted for a military career and carrying it out happily, found their families in want, and they reacted sharply by forming organizations dedicated to revolution against control of the government by politicians. Colonel Tojo was a member of the Control faction, which believed in working through the civil government. Yamashita declined to become involved. He was approached by the Action faction to give money to finance the rebellion within the army, but refused gently, saying he might sympathize with their feeling about the abuses in the system, but he would not subscribe to rebellion. Thus Yamashita antagonized both sides in this intra-army quarrel.

Late in the 1920s army politics led Prime Minister General Tanaka to try to take over Manchuria. The army was ready to do so, and even set up the murder of Zhang Zolin, the warlord of Manchuria, who had been sympathetic to Japanese ambitions but was turning away from them. Only fear that the Western powers would intervene if the Japanese moved stopped the army from trying a coup in Manchuria, but three years later the Kwantung Army did stage a coup and wrenched Manchuria away from China to become the puppet state of Manchukuo. This was followed by Japanese incursions into North China with the eye to establishing a separate government there also. Colonel Tojo was deeply involved in all these events but Colonel Yamashita still refused to play politics and thus incurred the personal animosity of his old friend. But because he firmly refused to join either faction, Colonel Yamashita was appointed chief of the Military Affairs Bureau, the section of the army that actually controlled internal army policies. The Military Affairs Bureau was responsible for national mobilization, national defense and military expenditure.

On the morning of February 26, 1936, young officers of the First Regiment led a rebellion, which they said was directed against corrupt political control of the government. Yamashita received a telephone call at home summoning him to the army minister's house. The young officers and their troops had already occupied the government buildings around the Imperial Palace and the residence of the prime minister. They tried to kill the prime minister but mistook his brother-in-law for the official and killed him instead. They occupied the police station opposite the Imperial Palace and their tanks patrolled the government district of Tokyo. They killed several of the Emperor's advisors.

At the ministry the young officers threatened War Minister

Rebel troops outside government buildings in Tokyo during the attempted coup of February 26, 1936.

Kawashima with death if he did not support their rebellion. The war minister asked for time to consult senior officers and summoned Yamashita. Together they went to the Imperial Palace where the minister had an audience with the Emperor. Hirohito was furious with the young officers. "They have cut off my arms and legs," he said of their murder of his officials. He demanded immediate action against them. Yamashita suggested that the Emperor order them back to their barracks but Hirohito refused to treat with the rebels.

Colonel Yamashita was known to be sympathetic to the young officers who had expressed such concern over the national welfare, but complete loyalty to the throne. The minister appointed him to deal with the rebels on behalf of the throne. The general officers were badly split, between those who wanted to sympathize with the rebellion and those who opposed their action, but all the generals tried to temporize until Hirohito threatened to lead the Imperial Guards personally from the palace to attack the rebels. He ordered the Tokyo garrison commander to move. Colonel Yamashita asked him to wait while he tried to resolve the matter. Some of the generals then became furious with Yamashita for trying to settle the affair on his own.

Ultimately the emperor took Yamashita's advice and ordered the young rebels back to their barracks. At the same time as the army command in Tokyo prepared to attack the rebels, they gave up and the primary ringleader shot himself.

Once the rebellion ended, the problem of the lesser figures of the revolt remained. Yamashita wanted to be lenient, because the rebellion had been carried out in what the young rebels thought was the public interest. Now they faced punishment but Yamashita wanted their loyalty to be emphasized. The other leaders offered to commit suicide if the emperor wished. The emperor refused to acknowledge their existence, and ultimately thirteen ringleaders were tried and executed secretly.

Yamashita decided to resign over this affair, but when he received a personal letter from the emperor asking him to stay on in the army he reconsidered. His friend General Hisaichi Terauchi also counseled him to remain. But they agreed that in dealing with the rebels Yamashita had made powerful enemies; several generals had asked him to intercede on behalf of the young officers and he had refused to go further because of the orders of the Emperor. Several other generals said he had gone too far in dealing with the rebels. The Emperor's military aide, General Honjo, had been deeply involved in the scandal, and his son-in-law had been one of the ringleaders. Honjo resigned as aide, and several other officers were forced to retire in disgrace because of their parts in the affair. Colonel Tojo was close to Honjo, who had earlier been commander of the Kwantung Army, and he was also jealous of Yamashita's role in the affair.

General Terauchi, who was one of the most powerful figures in the Control faction of the army, said it would be best
for Yamashita to get out of Tokyo for a while. Yamashita
was promoted to major general and assigned to the command at Seoul in Korea, which had been taken over as a
Japanese colony in 1910. Eighteen months later General
Yamashita was brought back to Tokyo and given command
of a division. By that time the war with China had broken
out and the division was sent to China, where it soon became
distinguished for its bravery, and its commander General
Yamashita as a commander who spent most of his time up
front with the troops. Yamashita's career in China was
marked by his usual efforts to maintain discipline and his
division was the most efficient and disciplined in the service.
His future in the army seemed to be assured.

2

Mission to Europe

By the time war broke out in Europe in the fall of 1939, the Imperial Army was deeply mired in China. The army had begun the campaign with high hopes. Their modern Japanese force, they thought, could not long be opposed by the outdated and inferior Chinese armies. But they were wrong. General Sugiyama, one of the cabal of generals who ran the army, had promised the Emperor that "the incident" would end in three months, but six months passed, and then a year, and every month the demands on Japan's economy grew greater.

The Japanese division bogged down in China and the Chinese Nationalist armies and the Communist guerrillas continued to fight on. The Communists in particular pinned down several divisions of troops in North China with the effective guerrilla tactics of the Eighth Route Army. The Japanese controlled the cities, and the railroads and highways by day, but any Japanese unit that moved out of garrison in less than column strength was likely to be ambushed. Thus Japan had gotten nowhere in the attempt to "pacify" China and bring it under Japanese influence. The Japanese—from the emperor down—dreamed of a united Asia, with Japan leading the other Asian nations out of Western colonialism, but the program was not working.

A principal reason was the conduct of the Japanese armies in the field, which was extremely arrogant from the top down. A new principle had been inserted into the command doctrine in this war: the commander of each region was solely responsible for civil and military affairs. He in turn delegated authority to his divisional and regimental commanders, who passed it down the line. Thus a captain who commanded a company ended up with life and death authority over his command area. The troops raped and murdered and looted civilians without any punishment. The commanding general would never hear of such incidents. Only when the scandal became so serious that it reached Tokyo would anything be done to rectify the situation. Usually this meant the selection of some junior officer as a "goat."

In the Rape of Nanking, for example, 250,000 Chinese soldiers and civilian men, women, and children were penned inside the city walls and abused and murdered for more than a month, and for this atrocity no one was punished.

This abnegation of command responsibility isolated the field generals. One of the results of the young officers' rebellion of 1936 had been to make the generals as a group begin to fear their younger officers and the officers recognized this and began to usurp command power. By 1938 it could be said that the majors and lieutenant colonels were running the army from staff positions. By 1938, while some semblance of control remained inside Japan, in the army-occupied areas abroad the Japanese army was running wild. In only a few sections, as with Yamashita's division in China, did the commanders maintain strict control of the behavior of their troops.

Instead of discipline, the militarists who controlled the army concerned themselves with the myth of Japanese invincibility that they were already building. The myth had received severe setbacks in two attacks by the Kwantung Army on the Soviets along the Mongolian border in 1938 and 1939. The Japanese had learned that their armor and air force were far inferior to that of the Russians. Where could they turn for assistance in modernizing their forces? That was a major question for the military planners in 1939.

When Japan had been asked by Hitler and Mussolini in 1939 to join the Rome-Berlin alliance in a treaty that was obviously designed to prevent the United States from entering the European war, there was considerable adverse reaction in Japan. Nonetheless the army almost universally favored the treaty. A few generals, like Yamashita, had qualms about it and felt that Japan should concentrate on her own problems and not get involved in an alliance against America.

After Japan signed the treaty of alliance with Germany and Japan on September 27, 1940, some of the generals suggested that a military mission be sent to Germany and Italy to study their methods. The navy concurred and asked to be represented as well.

But who was to head the mission? General Terauchi suggested that it be General Yamashita. The suggestion met with general favor, since Yamashita had proved himself beyond doubt in the field, as well as in general staff positions. One person who opposed the appointment was General Hideki Tojo, Yamashita's old travelling companion from Switzerland days. Tojo had now been advanced to a position of importance in army politics as war minister, because the ruling clique regarded him as a willing servant. He looked upon Yamashita as his only potential rival and did not want to advance Yamashita's cause in any way.

The pressure to make the Yamashita appointment, in which the emperor joined, was ultimately too great for Tojo to withstand. Yamashita's appointment was confirmed. In November, accompanied by an entourage of generals and

General Yamashita (center) at a conference with German generals
before the Second World War.

admirals, General Yamashita set off for Germany with the
title Inspector General of the Army Air Force.

When the mission arrived in Berlin, it was greeted with
honors by Hitler. It soon became evident that the German
dictator wanted the Japanese to enter the European war.
When Yamashita did not indicate interest in the prospect
Hitler lost interest in the commission and turned the man-
agement of the tour over to Reichsmarschal Hermann Goering, with instructions that the Japanese were not to be shown
too much.

Goering wined and dined the Japanese delegation, a task
at which he was a master. But every time they expressed a
desire to study some sensitive area, the conversation was
steered in another direction. In this autumn of 1940 the Germans had switched from an attempt to invade Britain to an

aerial bombardment campaign aimed at destroying the people's will to continue the war. The Japanese traveled to General Kesselring's headquarters in the Pas de Calais and visited the airfields to see the German armadas take off. The Luftwaffe officers boasted of victory, but General Yamashita was not fooled by the propaganda. He realized that Luftwaffe morale was low, and that the Nazis must be losing the campaign against the British. The Germans did show their aircraft to the visitors and Yamashita saw that the Nazis had not progressed as far in aircraft design as the Japanese had thought. The JU87 Stuka dive bomber had proved too slow and vulnerable for attack on cities and had been withdrawn from the air battle. The ME109 fighter was inferior to the Zero and so was the Focke-Wulff 190. The ME110 was most effective as a light bomber, not as a fighter. The mission learned nothing from the Germans about heavy bombers, because the Nazi air force did not have any, nor any program that involved them. Instead it depended on its JU88 bombers, which were no better than Japan's twin-engined medium bombers.

But what the Germans did have was a radar system in the developmental stage. It was nowhere near as effective as the British radar, but much more advanced than Japan's, which was primitive. Yamashita really wanted the secrets of radar and made inquiries several times. But Hitler was not willing for the secrets to be divulged and so Goering stalled every time the subject was mentioned. Finally Yamashita resorted to subterfuge.

The arrival of the commission had been widely publicized by the Nazis and every important German officer was familiar with it. But most did not know that Goering was trying to control the commission's activity. So one day, Yamashita sent his chief of staff to a lonely outpost near the Baltic, while he went off on one of Goering's tours. His chief of staff and assistants arrived at the secret headquarters of the experimental radar station and implied that they had been invited to inspect the facilities. The Germans turned out everything for them, and the Japanese took copious notes. At the end of the day they had what they wanted—a plan for a procedure to perfect their own radar on the German model.

The Germans offered the Japanese the new torpedo they had developed to replace their own imperfect model, whose exploders varied and sometimes did not function. But the Japanese navy did not need it. That navy already had the most highly developed and efficient torpedo in the world.

Everyone in the world knew that the Germans had developed a new concept of armored warfare, the Blitzkrieg, by which they had conquered Poland in two weeks and swept through France that spring of 1940. But the world did not know the techniques used, and these became a special study of the Yamashita commission. Yamashita soon learned that Japan's tanks were completely unsuitable for this type of warfare and new ones would have to be developed. The infantry would also have to learn to operate with tanks and tactical air support. The general also saw in the Luftwaffe and the British Royal Air Force the wave of the future.

The commission moved on to Italy in April 1941 but had scarcely begun its studies in June when a hurried call came from Berlin asking the return of the group to that city. Something important was about to happen. The naval contingent did not choose to believe the warning and continued its observations in Italy. When the army members arrived in Berlin Goering told them they should leave immediately for Japan if they wished to travel the Trans-Siberian railroad. The Russians were preparing to attack Germany, he said. It could happen any day.

Yamashita heeded the warning and put the army members of the commission on the train for Moscow the next day. As the train neared the Polish border with Russia they observed an enormous buildup of men and weapons. Clearly it was not the Russians who were about to attack Hitler, but the reverse. Operation Barbarossa was about to begin.

When the Japanese arrived in Moscow on June 20 they were greeted civilly but coolly and were not asked to call on Stalin. The Russians still distrusted Japan's ambitions in Siberia and Mongolia. Marshal Zhukov, who headed the welcoming committee, had been the commander of the Soviet armies in the Far East in 1938 and 1939 and had personally led the expedition against the Japanese when they attacked at Nomonhon in the summer of 1939, and had defeated the Kwantung Army so decisively that the emperor had intervened. Zhukov had since been promoted to assistant commissar of defense and there was a warning in his selection to greet the Japanese. General Yamashita observed that, and said nothing about what the Japanese had seen en route to Russia. They were not asked to linger in Moscow and took the eastbound train on the same day as their arrival. A few hours later they learned that the German attack on Russia had begun.

When the train reached Manchuria the Japanese alighted and proceeded to Port Arthur (Dalian) to await transportation to Japan. Yamashita called his people together and warned them against overrating the value of the alliance with Germany and Italy. He knew they had all been subjected to intensive German propaganda encouraging them to work for closer ties with the Axis, but he warned against it. Under no circumstances was their report to recommend war with the United States and Britain, he said. That could be suicidal. Japan must have time to rebuild its defense system and must be continually on guard against aggressive action from Russia. The fact that the Russians were now otherwise engaged with Germany did not alter the situation.

Two weeks later the army members of the commission were back in Tokyo. Since the naval contingent had been stranded in Italy and had to return by sea from Lisbon, the army group prepared a separate report. The report caused a sensation in army circles. Most officers, including War Minister Tojo, were vehemently opposed to the creation of a separate air force because it would cost the army control of its own air operations. Also, because the army had no love for the navy, unification of the forces was repugnant to the army high command. The navy was opposed for the same reasons. The old enmities were so strong that the unification plan could not get started, even though Yamashita argued that the conflicts and duplication of effort of the present system could mean Japan's defeat in war. Another recommendation, preparation for a large-scale war against Russia, was also ignored because of current preparations for war against the West. Yamashita specifically warned against such a war.

The Yamashita report also argued that the army should yield to the foreign ministry in conduct of foreign relations, and that the various arms of government should work toward a united front. That, too, was anathema to the army, which had begun the process of taking over the official relationships with China, Manchukuo, and French Indo-China. Later the Army would insist on the establishment of a Greater East Asia Ministry, which would be under army influence, and on that issue Foreign Minister Togo resigned.

War Minister Tojo elected to ignore the Yamashita Report and convinced Prime Minister that it should be tabled. The emperor then asked Yamashita for a special report of his findings. Then, in mid-October, the Konoye cabinet collapsed and General Tojo formed a new government. A considerable segment of the army command suggested that Yamashita should be appointed War Minister but when Tojo learned that, he elected to keep the War Ministry for himself, and lost no time in eliminating the man he considered to be his principal rival for power. He turned to Yamashita's contention that Japan must prepare for war against Russia. General Yamashita, said War Minister Tojo, was just the man to supervise the preparations. Yamashita was preparing the report for the emperor in November 1941 when orders were issued by General Sugiyama setting up a new command in Manchuria and assigning Yamashita to head it.

At the same time, General Terauchi was given command of all the troops in the southern area and sent to Saigon to supervise the coming war against the British and the Dutch. General Noyuboshi Muto, chief of the army bureau of military affairs, was soon transferred to a field command. These two generals and General Sugiyama comprised the cabal that had run the army up to now. So General Tojo, the figure they had created, had triumphed over two of them and only General Sugiyama stood between Tojo and absolute power. Sugiyama, as it turned out, was scheming as silently and carefully as Tojo. Soon he had the army operating at arm's length from the war ministry and Tojo found that he was informed about army affairs after they happened. This challenge to his power now became Tojo's major cause for concern and action. His old friend General Yamashita was well out of the way—in exile in Manchuria.

3

The Tiger of Malaya

One of the unusual practices of the Japanese Imperial Army of the 1940s was to select a field commander and throw him into action with virtually no time to prepare himself either for the troops he would lead or the area of operations. The army high command assumed that a general officer could do anything anywhere, and if he failed because of circumstance or bad planning he was held completely responsible.

This was precisely what happened to General Yamashita in 1941. He had scarcely gotten used to the Manchuria climate in that same month of November when he was ordered to Tokyo. From Saigon, General Terauchi had triumphed over General Tojo. Terauchi had recommended Yamashita for a field command in the south and General Sugiyama had acceded. There was really nothing Tojo could do to stop it without creating a crisis inside the army.

Yamashita was told that the army war plan against the West had been approved and he was to lead the troops in the initial assault on Malaya and Singapore. His new command was the Twenty-fifth Army, which consisted of the Fifth, Eighteenth, and Imperial Guards divisions, with the Fifty-sixth division in reserve. That army had begun training for amphibious operations on the Inland Sea and had recently been moved for training to the large island of Hainan, off the south China coast. That island was taken over by the Japanese army as an amphibious training center.

Yamashita was still wearing his heavy Manchurian uniform when he flew to Hainan to take command of an operation about which he knew nothing. In the Japanese fashion all the planning had been done by the staff of the army. The Malaya attack was to be the major opening land operation of the war. After the initial attacks on Malaya, Hong Kong, and the Philippines, the army would move into the Dutch East Indies and secure its petroleum supply. The army plans of conquest included the islands of the South Pacific, New Guinea, and then Australia. But the key to the whole army operation was the British fortress of Singapore. Until Singapore was captured the whole Japanese "strike South" plan was at risk.

The attack on Singapore would begin with assaults on the Kra Isthmus, which connected Thailand and Malaya. Two of the landing beaches, Singora and Pattani, were in Thailand, and one, Khota Baru, was in Malaya. Each of them was near an airfield. Imperial Headquarters had made all the plans; the major landing would be at Singora. The fact that Singora was in Thailand, and attack there involved violating the neutrality of that country, made not a whit of difference to Tokyo. The Thai would let them pass or the Thai would be subjugated.

Yamashita found that he had 24,000 men in the Fifth and Eighteenth divisions that would make the landings, and that these would be joined by the Imperial Guards division which would march from Indo-China across Thailand. That meant 36,000 men, with the 56th division in reserve aboard ship, to be called on if necessary. Yamashita was expected to capture Singapore and Malaya with this force, although he faced a British defense army of more than 100,000 men. Imperial

Headquarters was counting on surprise, a large naval attack force, and air support to carry the troops to victory.

In Tokyo Yamashita conferred for six days with Imperial Headquarters planners. Afterwards he flew to Taiwan, and then to Southern Army headquarters at Saigon, where he reported to General Terauchi, overall commander of the troops in the south.

More conferences were held in Saigon with Terauchi and Admiral Ozawa, head of the force that would land the troops and protect them in the first hours of the assault. The naval air force commander was also involved in these meetings. After three more days of conferences with higher authority and cooperating units, he held three days of meetings with the staffs of his divisions, and then he left for Hainan. There he found his divisions embarking on transports. Soon he boarded his command ship, the *Ryujo Maru*. She was a steamer fitted out with special communications equipment. He waited aboard her for the official word that the Pearl Harbor attack, the opening move of the war, was proceeding on schedule and would come on December 8. The attack on Malaya would come at about the same time, but if the Pearl Harbor attack was called off, the whole war effort would be scrubbed.

On November 30 the word came: the Pearl Harbor attack was scheduled. All that could stop the war now would be an eleventh-hour callback. General Yamashita stayed in his cabin aboard the ship and planned his attacks. He found that despite all the careful planning in Tokyo he had no maps of Malaya, and secured some school atlases which had very small-scale maps. These would have to do, at least for the initial phases. As for Singapore, he had no maps at all, and would have to depend on capturing some from the enemy.

The Japanese invasion force sailed on December 4: twenty small transports of about 10,000 tons each, with two cruisers and ten destroyers, and submarines scouting ahead of the convoy.

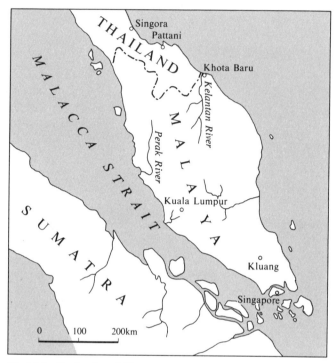

The Malay Peninsula and Singapore

The British were aware of the movement, and an alert was called in Singapore. Two days later the convoy was "snooped" by British scout planes. It altered course, to pretend that the troops would land in Indo-China. When informed of this move, the commander-in-chief of Malaya, Sir Robert Brooke-Popham, decided that the Japanese were simply carrying out maneuvers in connection with the China war and that there was no danger to his command.

Three years earlier, General Sir Arthur Percival, commander of the ground forces, had drawn up the original plan for defense of Malaya and Singapore, called Operation Matador. It presumed landings just where the Japanese would make them. But to defend against the landings, the British would have to violate Thailand's neutrality and that they were loath to do. So when the news of the course change of the convoy reached Singapore, Brooke-Popham put the Matador plan back in the safe. The plan had never been approved in London and now he failed to call London to get permission to activate it and cross Thai territory.

The Japanese invasion fleet changed course again, and on the night of December 7 was in position to land off Singora. The landings began. The Eleventh Indian Division, which was supposed to move into position to repel them, had not moved an inch from its barracks area, because of Brooke-Popham's decision to wait.

But there was resistance from the Thai, who did not like the Japanese crossing their territory, and began to fight. But their resistance lasted only a few hours, until orders came from Bangkok that the Thai were to join the Japanese as allies.

The Singora phase of the invasion was successful. The Pattani landings were unopposed. The Imperial Guards Division was marching across Thailand. Only at Khota Baru were the Japanese running into trouble. There the RAF had sunk one of the transports. The Indian troops manning the defenses of Khota Baru fought, but not very skillfully, and General Yamashita later said of the Indians that their tendency when confronted by Japanese soldiers was to run away into the jungle. But some of the Indians fought valiantly and died. By morning the fighting was violent and the Japanese were suffering heavy losses. Then the British muddled their communications and withdrew their aircraft from the Khota Baru airfield in the mistaken belief that it was about to be captured. Within the hour Japanese planes began to land on the first captured airfield.

The British commander, Brooke-Popham, radiated confidence as the struggle began. "Our defenses are strong and efficient and our preparations are made and tested," he cabled London.

Unfortunately for the defense none of those statements was true.

The defense forces consisted mostly of British, Indian, and Australian troops. The Indians, from the British Indian Army, had not received adequate training. They had been impressed in the last few months by a Japanese propaganda campaign directed against them specifically by radio and word of mouth. The Japanese army was invincible, the propagandists claimed, and there was nothing to be gained by fighting against it except death.

Nor had the defenses of Malaya and Singapore been tested against attack from the north, over land. The whole Singapore defense strategy had been laid in anticipation of an assault from the sea.

General Percival, the land commander, was much more realistic.

"Within twenty-four hours of the opening of the campaign, the Japanese gained their first objective, but at considerable cost," he reported to London. "Forces landed at the Kelantan River consist of rather less than one Japanese division."

Actually nearly two Japanese divisions were ashore and driving south. But many Japanese troops were left lying dead on the beaches because there was no time to bury them. British bombing had cost many of these lives but one incident bothered Yamashita more. A landing barge with two officers and thirty men aboard had disappeared. The men had deserted and were found four hundred miles away a few days later. Here was the first indication that despite all its claims the new Imperial Army was not well disciplined. Those officers and men were caught by the military police (*kempeitai*), taken to General Terauchi's headquarters in Saigon, tried and sentenced to prison terms. Yamashita would have tried them summarily and had them shot for desertion.

The Japanese drove swiftly south. General Percival noted after two days that the Japanese were "fighting efficiently and with great resourcefulness." The Indians tended to panic and the British left many vehicles behind, which was a boon to the Japanese, who had not brought very many trucks with them. Soon they were moving units along the road in British trucks.

One of Yamashita's major problems was the behavior of his own troops. They were out of control, mistreating the local people, seizing food and supplies and murdering and raping. Yamashita ordered the chief of the political section of the army to take strong action against such behavior. He wanted his troops to make Japan proud by behaving with dignity. He was distressed that they did not seem to know how. The junior officers were largely responsible for this breakdown in discipline. They heard the orders of their superiors, and did precisely as they wished. The result was a cruelty and disregard of human rights for which the Japanese army was already notorious in China and now would make that army infamous everywhere it went.

This ambience was all a result of planned army policy. After the army seized power in 1937 the Imperial Army changed completely. When General Sadao Araki became the Minister of Education that year, he began to turn the schools into instruments of the army. Pupils had always bowed to the Imperial portrait that hung in every school; now they were forced to pray to the photograph of the god-emperor every morning when the Red Sun flag was run up on the school flagpole in a military-style ceremony, and the national anthem became a holy chant. Middle school students were taught to drill and given the fundamentals of military discipline, foremost of which was immediate obedience to any orders given by an immediate superior. They were taught the beginnings of the new *bushido*. As vice minister of war General Tojo had devised a book for the instruction of the army which was built around the principle of emperor worship and glorification of death in battle for the emperor. Tojo's book became a school handbook.

When the boys left high school and became soldiers they were subjected to a new sort of military discipline, calculated cruelty by their noncommissioned officer superiors that was designed to break their spirit and make them totally obedient. They were thus deprived of the advantages of civilization that their political leaders had sought to instil. Most commanding generals found themselves kept aloof from their troops by the colonels and lieutenant colonels of the staff. This was the situation in which General Yamashita now found himself, in an army that had changed so much since he had left the command of troops to go to Europe that he did not recognize it.

Yamashita's staff tried to keep him from contact with the troops on the pretense of saving him from petty detail. He was responsible to Imperial General Headquarters for victory, but other than that Imperial General Headquarters had no interest in what went on at the divisional and regimental level. Thus the regimental and divisional commanders had complete control of the areas in which they operated, and innumerable atrocities and cruelties came out of this abandonment of military law by the high command. In the ranks, the concept of emperor worship was carried to the extreme. Ultimately men were ordered to die for the emperor in suicide operations and if they objected they were the first to be sent to their deaths. In the American army, as an example of the differences, when General George Patton, as an army commander, slapped the face of a soldier, his career very nearly came to an end. He was forced to apologize to the soldier, and was denied command for many months. The entire American army learned of the incident, and it served as an example to officers. A Japanese officer could shoot one of his soldiers for some dereliction of duty and Yamashita would never hear of it.

In the Malayan attack, Yamashita found that he had difficulty with his Twenty-fifth Army command at several levels. One was technical; his communications were so faulty that he was often out of touch with his division commanders. But more important, he found his troop units difficult to control. The Imperial Guards were the worst. When they joined the fighting after the first few days. Yamashita found that they wanted to do things their own way, and objected to interference from above. To get them to obey orders he had to make an issue of every order.

But luckily for Yamashita, the British forces were crumbling in his path, and the Fifth and Eighteenth Japanese divisions were more or less under control. Two weeks after the invasion, the Japanese had captured all of Malaya above the Perak River, and had control of the railroad that ran south to Singapore.

The speed of the Japanese campaign so alarmed the British in London that Air Chief Marshal Brooke-Popham was relieved of command of the defense and authority was put in the hands of Field Marshal Earl Wavell, who was responsible for the whole southwest Pacific.

The change in command made little difference in the campaign. Yamashita was moving so fast he outran his supply train. Over the opposition of his staff, he improvised another landing using barges and small boats. The staff officers resented his assumption of actual command. Particularly opposed was Colonel Masanori Tsuji, an officer who had come direct from Imperial General Headquarters. Tsuji tried to scuttle the planned landings and communicated his attitude to the junior officers, who carried out their orders in a half-hearted and sloppy fashion. The landings were made in the wrong place, the landing force did not make contact with

General Yamashita addressing his troops during the invasion of Malaya and Singapore.

the major force, and the result was 1500 Japanese soldiers floundering in the jungle behind the British lines. But the British were confounded by the landing operation, which they could not understand, and believed that Yamashita was up to some devious and deadly maneuver. So the result was more salutary that Yamashita expected.

The British made a stand at the Slim River to protect Kuala Lumpur. The Japanese attacked and won a victory after nineteen hours of battle and then began to drive south even more rapidly. The British retreat became a rout and the Japanese captured enough guns, ammunition, and food to keep them going for a month.

But Yamashita still faced more problems within his own force. Colonel Tsuji insisted that he had been right in opposing the motorboat landings, and became more argumentative. Yamashita had to discipline a front-line battalion commander—a personal friend—because of atrocities committed by his troops at the Slim River battle and Tsuji objected. In any other army Tsuji would have been disciplined for this flouting of authority, but since he represented Imperial General Headquarters, Yamashita simply ignored him.

In his diary Yamashita noted his dissatisfaction with the state of army discipline: "We still have many things to do among ourselves. Our education and outlook are not what they should be. We must encourage the sort of outlook that will make us proud of our nation. Those who have come to Malaya without this outlook may be debased. This is one of the things I must keep a careful watch over."

Another problem was the reluctance and sometimes refusal of his officers to obey his orders. This was a constant struggle.

Overall, the campaign was going so well that just before the drive on Singapore began, Yamashita released his reserve Fifty-sixth division to go to Burma because he did not need it. The British defense was decaying so rapidly that he was confident of victory with his 36,000 troops, even though the enemy numbered three times his force.

A pitched battle was fought at the Muar River, and the struggle was violent. In the end the Japanese triumphed and then the Imperial Guards division committed the worst atrocities of the campaign, killing wounded soldiers as they lay on the field, and beheading two hundred of them.

The Imperial Guards had become so unruly that when a regimental commander was wounded, Yamashita did not give the Guards commander the usual honor of selecting his successor but did so himself, to find a man who would obey his orders.

General Nishimura, commander of the Imperial Guards division, insisted that his troops should lead the attack on Singapore, but Yamashita did not trust them and instead chose the other two divisions, which he felt he could control. Nishimura was furious and went into a sulk. Yamashita ignored him and moved ahead, although he was fearfully short of supplies and ran the danger of running out altogether if the campaign lasted much longer.

On January 25, after the last defensive position on the Muar River was abandoned by the British, Field Marshal Wavell authorized General Percival to retreat to Singapore. Here the British expected to hold. Brooke-Popham had said Singapore could withstand siege for years with its great fixed guns surrounding the harbor and the base. But the problem was that the guns were turned seaward, for no one had ever anticipated an overland attack down the narrow peninsula.

Near the end of January, forty-eight Hurricane fighters were delivered to Singapore to bolster the defenses, but on January 28 the Japanese cut off the Twenty-second Indian brigade south of Kluang, and three days later the last ragged remnants of the British defense were withdrawn across the narrow strait to Singapore island. The siege was about to begin. Standing on the bank opposite the island bastion, General Yamashita called for the surrender of Singapore, but the call was rejected scornfully. General Yamashita was faced with a real crisis. He had supplies left for no more than a week, a matter carefully concealed from the British. If he did not take Singapore in a hurry he would have to withdraw and the battle would be lost.

On February 8 Yamashita authorized the use of most of his remaining artillery ammunition in a heavy bombardment of Singapore. As darkness came the Fifth and Eighteenth divisions crossed the strait, followed by the reluctant Imperial Guards. They landed in the northwest sector of the island, which was defended by the Twenty-second Australian brigade.

From the outset the fighting was murderous. The Australians stood their ground, although they were hampered by lack of artillery. The big guns of Singapore were of virtually no use to them, with their silent muzzles pointing out to sea. The garrison of the island now roused itself for defense along the Jurong line, 85,000 strong, opposing Yamashita's 36,000.

The Australians continued their brave defense, but were undercut by the ineptitude of the command. Confusion in orders caused General Percival to sacrifice valuable territory. The Australians were ordered quite needlessly to evacuate part of the Jurong line, and the Japanese rushed in. On February 11, the British forces were pushed back, the Australians counterattacked, and the Japanese drove them back with heavy losses. The British line then pulled back to the final perimeter around the town of Singapore.

General Yamashita was now nearly desperate for food and ammunition. But so too were the British in trouble, short of ammunition and water, because the Japanese held the reservoir. Once again, Yamashita called on the British to surrender, indicating that if they did not, his strength was such that he could destroy them. General Percival asked for terms. Yamashita, his heart in his mouth, said, "I have one question. Will you surrender, yes or no?"

The bluff worked. Percival surrendered his force of 85,000 to Yamashita's three divisions. It was one of the greatest and swiftest victories in history. At the outset, Imperial General Headquarters gave Yamashita 100 days to take Singapore. He conquered Britain's greatest Asian naval base, "the Gibraltar of the Pacific" in 70 days with a loss of fewer than 10,000 men, mostly in the beginning of the cam-

Former Prime Minister Hideki Tojo testifies during the Tokyo War Crimes Trials.

paign. The British lost 138,000 men in this worst disaster in British history.

Tokyo was agog. The emperor could not believe that his troops had scored such a triumph. The white man had been debased, trampled into the dirt for the first time. The illusion of superiority was transmitted from the army to all Japan, and the people began to believe the army propaganda that the Japanese were a race of supermen. Some wise heads counseled that now was the perfect opportunity to call for peace and secure the resources that Japan needed, but even the emperor was now infected and the opportunity allowed to slip by.

The Twenty Fifth Army was honored by the emperor for its victory, all except the Guards division, which had disgraced itself by atrocities and refusal to obey orders. General Nishimura was relieved of command and the division was broken up when it returned to Japan.

General Yamashita was mentioned in the Imperial Rescript celebrating the victory. He was called "The Tiger of Malaya" and his name was on every Japanese lip. He might have expected a triumphal return to Tokyo and the imperial reception accorded every victorious general, but Prime Minister General Tojo intervened. On the pretext of military necessity he persuaded General Sugiyama to send Yamashita directly from Malaya to Manchuria to assume a new command facing the Russians. As long as Tojo remained in power the man he considered his major rival would be kept in exile.

This exile lasted two years, while Tojo and the army he had turned into a monster proceeded to lose the war. The end came in sight in June 1944 when the Americans invaded the Marianas islands and captured Saipan, Tinian, and Guam. This victory gave them a series of operating bases for their B-29 heavy bombers, which for nearly two years had been working against Japan ineffectually from west China bases.

The fall of Saipan caused the downfall of Tojo in July 1944. The Marianas islands were considered to be part of Japan's inner defenses and when they were lost so was the emperor's confidence in Tojo, who had promised that Japan would not be bombed. Months earlier Tojo had lost his support within the army by a series of maneuvers designed to give him total power. So in fact no one was sorry to see Tojo's fall. Hardly had he resigned as prime minister than General Yamashita was returned from exile to take on a task even more difficult and thankless than the invasion of Malaya. Imperial General Headquarters asked him to revitalize the defense of the Philippines. There was much talk about "victory" but in their hearts the generals knew that Yamashita was being asked to fight a delaying action, to stall the American advance so it would take months to reach Japan. The forlorn hope now was that the Americans could be made to suffer such heavy losses that they would lose heart for the invasion of the Japanese home islands and settle for a negotiated peace.

From the outset General Yamashita knew that this strategy was nonsense and when he left Japan for the Philippines it was with a sense of doom. He did not expect to see his family or his homeland again.

4

The End of a National Hero

General Yamashita arrived in the Philippines in October 1944 and he immediately began to reorganize the command and instil military discipline within his army. Including naval troops who came under his overall orders, he had more than 430,000 men, but shortages of equipment, food, and ammunition.

As he had feared from what he had learned in the briefings in Tokyo he faced a serious problem with the civil population because of the behavior of the previous command. But there was no time to reeducate his troops or to try to convince the Filipinos that the Japanese meant them well. He had to adopt the principle that those who were opposed to the Japanese were their enemies. In 1942 the Americans had managed to establish guerrilla operations in the Philippines, and the conduct of the Japanese army in the islands had driven thousands of Filipinos either to join or support the guerrillas. After looking into the situation, Yamashita commented: "In the Philippines the war has come to a situation of kill or be killed. No matter what the person is, a Filipino or not, if we hesitate we ourselves will be killed." So it was win or lose and the devil be damned.

When 130,000 American troops from the advance base at

Ulithi landed at the end of October 1944, they hit the island of Leyte first, as Yamashita had expected. He had planned a defense there with about sixty thousand men. Yamashita's plan called for them to defend the island while Yamashita himself supervised a buildup of the defense of Luzon. But he was ordered by Imperial General Headquarters to put more troops into Leyte to defeat the Americans and the order was confirmed when he met with Field Marshal Terauchi, who had moved his headquarters from Saigon to Singapore, and then to Manila. Terauchi said the order came directly from the emperor. This was not true; the order was engendered as part of the Sho Plan, a desperate attempt to turn the war around.

Under the Sho Plan the navy was to divide the remnants of the Combined Fleet into four units. The First Striking Force, commanded by Admiral Shoji Nishimura, would steam through the Sibuyan Sea to Surigao Strait, whereupon it would turn north and annihilate the American ships standing off the beaches of Leyte. This force would be followed by the Second Striking Force, commanded by Rear Admiral Kiyohide Shima, which would join in the action. The Center Force, commanded by Admiral Takeo Kurita, would move through San Bernardino strait between Luzon and Samar islands and come down from the north, to enclose the American naval forces in a pincers. The fourth force, consisting of all the aircraft carriers Japan now possessed, would move north of Luzon island to entice Admiral William F. Halsey's American Third Fleet away from Leyte. This naval effort was supposed to produce the "decisive battle" the Japanese had been seeking since Pearl Harbor. It would be supported by the Japanese naval and army air forces while the land army defeated the Americans and drove them into the sea. Compelled to participate in this plan because of the growing insanity of Imperial General Headquarters, General Yamashita had to conduct a defense in which he did not believe. He was forced to send reinforcements to Leyte, most of which did not ever arrive, their ships sunk by allied air and naval action. The naval forces were almost completely sacrificed.

Soon the Japanese Army on Leyte was reduced to starvation because of the impossibility of getting supplies through the allied cordon.Yamashita wanted to abandon Leyte but Terauchi would not have it. But Terauchi, too, knew that the Battle of the Philippines was going to end in disaster and he soon moved his headquarters back to Saigon. From there, following orders from Tokyo he kept interfering with Yamashita's conduct of the defense of the Philippines. He insisted that Leyte be defended to the death of every Japanese soldier and that reserves from Luzon be poured in. Thousands of men were sent, but when the end came early in 1945 there were only 13,000 Japanese left alive on Leyte. The defense had been useless and a complete waste of manpower.

From the outset General Yamashita had not wanted to defend Manila. He knew he could not win the struggle against the allies. His intention was to fight a delaying action for as long as possible, hoping to wear down the Americans and hoping that events elsewhere would push the enemy into giving Japan an acceptable peace. Manila's only value to him was the harbor, and if that was destroyed, then the million inhabitants of Manila would prove to be an enormous responsibility and liability. Consequently he planned from the beginning to move the central defense to the mountains of Luzon. Yet Manila was defended, against Yamashita's orders, by a force of about 20,000 naval troops under Admiral Iwabachi, who had decided on his own to stage a battle to the death. Japanese communications by the end of 1944 were completely disrupted and General Yamashita was unaware of the furious battle raging there for ten days. When he learned he ordered Iwabachi to withdraw, an order that was not obeyed. The Japanese navy added to the horrors committed by the army by carrying on a campaign of rape and murder in Manila in the last days.

On Luzon General Yamashita's force retreated steadily into the jungle and finally to the almost unexplored area of the Asin River. On June 26 Japanese forces left the Cagayan area of Luzon. and this was the end of really organized resistance, although Yamashita kept fighting. He established his final headquarters in the mountains north of Manila. Until the end he attempted to maintain discipline over his troops, and when the Russians entered the war in August, he warned his men that they must maintain discipline "and do your best to save the honor of the Japanese Army. All of you will have chance to perform your last service to your country."

When the war ended on August 15, Yamashita ordered his troops to rescue civilians and the sick from the mountains and to try to keep alive. Some of his officers suggested that he kill himself to save capture by the Americans but he refused. Who would take the responsibility if he died? He determined to stay on and take what came to him.

On August 19 an order came by radio from Field Marshal Terauchi ordering the Fourteenth Army to stop fighting but not to surrender. Terauchi said he would send a staff officer to supervise the surrender. He wanted to know the name of an airfield to which the officer might be sent. The order showed how little Terauchi knew in these last days about the situation in the Philippines. Yamashita had not controlled an airfield for several weeks.

So General Yamashita responded to an American request (made by leaflet) that he surrender and sent an officer to the American lines with a white flag and a letter. On the morning of September 2, 1945, General Yamashita walked down a jungle trail to the American lines at Kiangan. He was driven to U.S. Army Headquarters, where he handed over his samurai sword and signed an instrument of surrender. Present at the surrender was General Percival, the commander of the British troops in Singapore, who had been liberated from a Japanese prison camp in the Philippines.

After the surrender Yamashita was informed that the Americans planned to try him for "war crimes." Despite that, Yamashita's enemies respected him. As American army historian Robert Ross Smith wrote, "No one can ever dispute that Yamashita executed one of the most effective delaying actions in the whole history of warfare." He had done his job impeccably. Now he would have to face victor's justice.

Beginning on October 29, 1945, General Yamashita was tried as a war criminal in Manila. He was charged with 123 counts involving the death of 57,000 people. Most of the charges stemmed from the defense of Manila, against his order, by the crazed naval contingent.

Stripped of all the verbiage, the real issue was the responsibility of a commanding general for all the actions committed by his troops. This was the first such indictment to come out of the Pacific War, and on the outcome would depend the fate of many other Japanese officials.

Yamashita's American defense lawyers, convinced of his personal innocence of war crimes, fought his case as well as they could, taking it to the United States Supreme Court and to President Harry Truman. But the prosecution insisted, without ever proving the point, that General Yamashita must have known about the atrocities because they were common knowledge among the Filipinos. The prosecutor did not give any credence to the fact that Yamashita was not in contact with Filipinos. Some of the atrocities for which he was tried were committed before he arrived in the Philippines. The prosecution did not ever prove any links between Yamashita and the atrocities. Their whole case was based on the assumption that Yamashita must have known what was happening at every level of his command, when in fact he did not.

Of the trial, British reporter Henry Keyes wrote in the

London Daily Express: "Yamashita's trial continued today—but it isn't a trial. I doubt if it is even a hearing. Yesterday his name was mentioned once. Today it was not brought up at all.

"The military commission sitting in judgement continued to act as if it were not bound by any laws or any rules of evidence. I have no brief for any Japanese, but in no British court of law would the accused receive such rough and ready treatment as has Yamashita."

Japanese officers testified that there was no general order for massacre, and Admiral Okochi, commander of naval forces in the southwest Pacific, said he had given the order for the destruction of Manila. General Umezu, the former chief of staff of the Japanese army, testified in Yamashita's behalf. But it all made no difference. The Americans were out to prove that Yamashita, as commander in the Philippines, was responsible for everything his forces did. They wanted to set a precedent so they could try many other officers. As for the atrocities, particularly those committed by the navy in Manila, Yamashita said, "Those bloody incidents which arose were utterly against my orders." And when the Americans asked him about "Orders from Tokyo" which were supposed to have included a plan to wipe out all the inhabitants of Manila, he said simply that he had 100,000 soldiers on Luzon and even if they had been fully engaged, it would have been impossible for them to murder a million people. There was no such order. The only destruction he had ordered was the blowing up of militarily important bridges. As for his policy toward prisoners of war, his orders were that they were to be treated exactly the same as Japanese officers and soldiers were treated.

But the defense came to nothing and at the end of thirty-two days of trial, as expected, Yamashita was found guilty of all the charges, and ordered to be hanged. Several dissenting justices of the U.S. Supreme Court said that Yamashita

had been convicted in a kangaroo court, and that the precedent set there might possibly boomerang against Americans
some day. But nobody was really listening. On the morning
of February 23, 1946, General Yamashita was hanged by his
victorious enemies.

Afterword

Togo, Yamamoto, and Yamashita and
the Influence of the West

World War I and the Treaty of Versailles should be regarded as a point of departure for Japan in the twentieth century. At that point, because of Western actions and Western attitudes, Japan's attitude towards the West changed. In the nineteenth century the Japanese had copied Western ways in seeking empire, only to find that when they became an imperial power the Westerners suspected their ambitions and contrived to frustrate Japanese expansion, as in the forced relinquishment of the Liaotung Peninsula after the China war of 1894, and the pressure of the U.S. at the Treaty of Portsmouth in 1905 that denied Japan the cash indemnity she so desperately needed after the Russo-Japanese War. From Tokyo these actions looked very much like a Western conspiracy to keep Japan down.

It is true that World War I offered Japan opportunity to increase her empire, but no more than it offered France and Britain, which gained territory and concessions at the expense of Germany in Africa, the Middle East, and in the Pacific. But the great shock of the war to Japan (and China) at Versailles was the realization that the West was going to ignore their basic demand to be treated as equals by their erstwhile Western partners. The Western powers proceeded to divide up the world and the loot of conquest as though the Asians had not been parties to the war. This shock played into the hands of the Japanese militarists and brought a major change in the Japanese approach to the West.

From the time of the Washington Naval Conference in 1921, the Imperial Japanese Navy separated into the Treaty and Fleet factions. The difference had not existed in the days of Togo or even in the early days of Yamamoto's career. The most competent naval officers concentrated on building the Imperial Navy as a fighting force. But in 1921 the Japanese learned that they were to be relegated to a position of inferiority to Britain and the U.S. in naval affairs. Some Japanese officers, like Yamamoto, could accept that at least temporarily, as a matter of need. Others could not.

The Versailles Treaty restored Shandong Province—the former German colony of Kiaochao—to China and returned power over Manchuria to China. Seeing their new gains stripped away angered the empire builders of Japan and caused them to accept the thesis that the white man must be driven from Asia if Japan was to secure the leadership of the region. One aspect of this ambition was the benign philosophical position that only Japan among Asian societies had been able to escape the white man's yoke, and thus only Japan could lead Asia out of colonialism. When criticized by those who said Japan was simply following the Western path to power and empire, these benign philosophers could say: Yes, but this is only temporary. As the Asian nations become prepared for freedom they shall have it, and in the end Japan shall lead a free Asia in the councils of the world.

In spite of their defeat in the Pacific War, the Japanese achieved this objective of driving the white man from domination of Asia. The Asians were awakened to demand self-government. In Indonesia the Japanese occupation was throughly enlightened toward the indigenous population although barbaric toward the Westerners. But the horrors, as everywhere, could be laid to Japanese army policy.

The navy became involved in this expansionism as a result of the British decision in the 1920s not to renew the Anglo-Japanese alliance. That decision was prompted by urgings from the United States. Australia and New Zealand both urged Britain to renew, but Canada, under American influence, urged the abandonment of the alliance. The American position in the 1920s derived largely from a racist view of the world that had been developing steadily since the 1870s. But the American position was given an enormous boost by the Japanese victory in the Russo-Japanese war and then the development of a powerful Japanese navy during World War I.

Faced with the emergence of a powerful Japan at the end of World War I, Britain chose to regard Japan as a competitor rather than a partner. This was a reaction to the new militancy of the Imperial Army. Besides cancelling the Anglo-Japanese Alliance, Britain decided to build the great Singapore Naval Base, which the Japanese saw as aimed at them alone. It was at this point that Admirals Kanji Kato and Suetsugu broke away from the main stream of Japanese naval thinking and advocated the building of a powerful Japanese navy to protect Japanese interests. As those interests changed to empire building, so did the Fleet faction of the navy adapt itself to the army's ambitions.

The Western limitation on Japanese naval armament had another effect in the 1920s and 1930s. In order to secure parity Japan's naval leaders were forced to take a new look at fleet doctrine. Out of this came the emergence of Japan as the world leader in naval aviation. The man most responsible for this was Admiral Yamamoto. He developed the best naval aircraft of his time and his unique creation of the multicarrier force was later copied in the west, particularly by the Americans. His use of the multi-engined seaplane as a naval search plane was also copied, although the West never did produce anything as effective as the Kawanishi flying boat. In all this Yamamoto was picking up where American General Billy Mitchell left off. The controversy over Mitchell's obsession with the potential of air power was raging when Yamamoto was naval attache in Washington.

The Japanese Army's ambitions were a combination of the Prussian influence and a logical outcome of the manner in which the Meiji era reformers of Japan established the constitutional monarchy, giving the military extraordinary powers, outside the framework of civilian government. In fact the military was never controlled by civilians. The navy, until the 1930s, accepted civil control, but the army never did, and had a history of bringing down governments, usually over the issue of the military budget, that went back to the original days of the restored monarchy. The Army was only really happy when a general was prime minister. From the days of Giichi Tanaka those generals were all empire builders, because after World War I there was no other justification for the maintenance of a large standing army and civilians were clamoring for armed force reduction and budget cutting. General Tanaka's answer in 1927 was to demand the annexation of Manchuria and North China to the Japanese empire, and thereafter the army policy never wavered. It was the fatal flaw of the Meiji Constitution to give special powers to the military that enabled the army to seize political power in 1937 and to maintain that power until defeated by the Western allies. This defect was remedied in 1947 with the adoption of the new Japanese Constitution establishing civilian control of the military and removing the emperor from any but symbolic contact.

To understand the attitudes of the Imperial Army one must remember its samurai background and the conditions under which modernization was undertaken. Whereas those samurai who elected to enter the navy were faced with a new way of doing everything, the samurai who elected to join the army found conditions relatively the same as they had been under the shogunate. To be sure this was a conscript army and they had to disabuse themselves of the notion that only the military caste was capable of fighting. But once they had done this, they brought many of the attitudes of the samurai with them into the service. The French and Germans, who trained them, had to insist on the abandonment of the samurai sword and the adoption of the Western military sabre.

After the earthquake of 1923 created havoc and financial crisis in Japan, the military authorities were forced to make reductions. They scrapped four divisions in 1925, but enlarged the army air force. The result was not much of a change and it did not last long. By 1931, using Manchuria as an excuse, the army was getting new divisions, most of which went to China and Manchuria. There was also a change in the armament of the Japanese army to an offensive rather than defensive capability. It was the claim of the generals that the reason was that a good offense is the best defense, but history records that this was not their primary objective. From the beginnings of the Kwantung Army, which in 1931 had only 12,000 men, the whole army was turned toward offensive capability and by 1937 it numbered half a million men. The army's enforcement of the principle of emperor worship. which was brought to the schools under Education Minister General Araki, turned Japan into a military camp. From the time that a child first attended school he or she was militarized. The whole of Japanese society was placed on a military footing in 1937 and the army was transformed. The new fake Bushido invented by War Minister Tojo replaced the old Meiji rescript to soldiers and sailors. Under the Meiji rescript the servicemen were told to be loyal and disciplined, to respect their enemies and to obey the orders of their superiors. The superiors were told to treat their inferiors with consideration "making kindness their chief aim." They should respect valor and should never despise their enemies.

All this was lost in Tojo's recreation of the army in a new image in 1937. Recruits were brutalized to the point of torture by their sergeants and corporals and they in turn took out their frustrations in brutalizing the people, first of China, and then of other Asian countries. Their junior officers told them never to surrender, and they were taught to despise any enemy who did surrender. From the samurai the Japanese inherited an arrogance that made them believe the Japanese was the best fighter in the world. The army encouraged this belief and the generals believed it themselves up until the day of defeat, and then, like the Prussian generals of World War I, they tried to shift the blame to the politicians.

After World War II, the entire military was disbanded, until the American occupation authorities learned that the Japanese had to have minimal defenses. The defense forces were recreated in the American image, adopting General Yamashita's recommendation for a separate air force. The Japanese went one step further, and created a common defense academy for all three services, with specialization coming after graduation. As for the schools, emperor worship, the singing of the national anthem and the flying of the national flag were forbidden for many years, and even half a century after the war they are unpopular with the left wing.

When General Douglas MacArthur came to Japan to head the occupation force, disarm Japan, and restructure Japanese society to prevent Japan from again becoming an aggressor nation, he succeeded far better than anyone realized at the time. The "MacArthur Constitution," pressed on Japan by the Americans, outlawed war altogther, and if that was a cynical bit of victor's justice, it had an effect so profound that some Americans now rue the day that it was imposed. Later, faced with difficulties in Asia, the Americans wanted the Japanese to rearm and to take much of the responsibility for defense of the Pacific region, only to find the Japanese people reluctant to do so. They have taken seriously the injunction against making war or even preparing for war.

The postwar restructuring of Japan also added another welcome element to Japanese society and government: the ultimate reestablishment of a Japanese Defense Agency under strict civilian control. The prime minister of Japan is chief of the Japanese armed forces. All three arms of defense are under the supervision of a civilian defense chief to whom the admirals and the generals report. All this bodes well for the future of Japan as a growingly democratic society.

Yet there continues to exist in Japan a nucleus of the old militarism and military disdain for civil government. The peculiar relationship of Tokyo's Yasukuni Shrine to the government continues. In deference to the wishes of some of their constituents, a long procession of ministers have made official and unofficial visits to this shrine dedicated to Japan's war dead, although such visits were outlawed during the American occupation. The shrine has never since regained its favored position, but there seems every reason to believe it receives covert support.

Every country has its way of honoring the war dead. There is no reason Japan should not do so, but the Yasukuni Shrine is linked with the whole question of Japan's war responsibility, which the government by the century's final decade still has not addressed openly. When that is done, the Yasukuni Shrine will have the same significance as the tombs of the unknown soldiers in Western nations and the overtones of militarism will vanish.

Japan's military tradition is older than the modern nation. Theoretically that tradition was wiped out in 1945, but actually it never ended; the United States found it impossible to administer a Japan that lacked a naval defense force, and the exigencies of world politics prompted the Americans to begin rebuilding the Japanese military in the 1950s and to put pressure on Japan to build faster than it wanted to. In the 1990s Japan has one of the half dozen most efficient military organizations in the world and one of the largest defense budgets.

What is the legitimate function of the Japanese military? The steady decrease in the American military presence in Asia will make Japan responsible for an increasing number of aspects of Asian security. In that projection, some brutal possibilities must be faced involving instability in Russia, China, and North Korea.

The attention of the world is on the United Nations and the attempts of its members to keep the peace through their military forces. But with the Balkans aflame, elements of the old Soviet Union still smoking, and Southeast Asia remaining a tinderbox, there is grave doubt as to the UN's ability to accomplish its noble task. One major power could decide to destroy the entire structure, and Japan cannot afford to be anything but watchful.

During the buildup of the Japanese Self-Defense Forces there were officials who lamented Japan's 1945 defeat quite openly. One such was Minoru Genda, closely associated with the air attack on Pearl Harbor, who ended his career as a general officer in the Air Self-Defense Force. There is also a historic tradition of analyzing what went wrong with one campaign and another as part of the curriculum of the defense institutions.

The 1990s Japan's defense is keyed to America's, but it must be remembered that until 1920, Japan's defense was keyed to Britain's. The American relationship might not always continue.

To recall the Versailles Treaty, conditions in the early 1990s resemble those of the early twentieth century. Yugoslavia was established at Versailles but after seventy years its component parts have unravelled. The whole Balkan area is much as it was before World War I. Czechoslovakia has come undone. Italy finds itself in a conditon of disunity. financial difficulty, and political corruption similar to that which brought on Fascism.

In Japan the degree of political corruption is as great as anywhere. This state of affairs is distressing to idealists and damaging to the national welfare. In the fall of 1992 Major Shinsaku Yanai, a lecturer in military history and strategy at the Japanese Defense Academy, published an article in the weekly magazine *Shukan Bunshun* calling for a military coup d'etat or a revolution to destroy the corrupt politicians who run Japan.

"It's now impossible to right the wrongs legally through elections, the basis of a democracy. What paths can we take to remove this? Only a coup d'etat or a revolution."

In the face of the almost daily evidence of the past few years no one can deny the pervasive corruption. But the major's call for a coup d'etat is reminiscent of the young officers' rebellion of February 26, 1936. Obviously the major was sincere, as he laid his career on the line, although he might not have anticipated the storm that followed. Defense Chief Sohei Miyashita rebuked him publicly, saying this view was Yanai's own and that although he expected the media to say that such thinking permeated the defense establishment, this charge would be untrue.

Perhaps. The evidence is not all in, but it is unlikely that within a group of hardworking young men and women who are dedicated to the preservation of their country, there are not many who feel that the Japanese political corruption of the 1990s has passed permissible bounds.

Still, the corruption of the body politic is the responsibility of the electorate, and would not be cured by a coup, as the rise and fall of the militarists indicates only too clearly. Japan has inherited from the West a growing sense of responsibility that may hold promise for a purge of the political system.

Similarly, the pressure on Japan to make amends to its Asian neighbors with a clear apology for its behavior in the 1930s and 1940s is growing in the 1990s. Soon the progress the Japanese people want may be made in settling the national position as a bastion of peace and stability.

Today, with the emergence of three new political parties dedicated to reform, Japan is moving closer to true democracy.

As to the charge that Japan has replaced military aggression with economic aggression, to a great extent that is the lament of those nations that cannot stand the competition. Among them is the United States, which chose in the 1960s to convert its economy from one based on production to one based on consumption and service. Only in the 1990s is an attempt being made to return to a production society.

But these complaints of economic aggression have a certain validity to which Japanese business and industry have been slow to respond. The foreign cry for more importation of consumer goods in the 1990s is being joined by the cries of the Japanese consumers who are beginning to demand more for their yen. This tendency is bound to increase as Japan moves to get in step with the rest of the world.

The process has been long and arduous. Admiral Togo was a man of his time, coming out of a feudal society into a world he had to help build. He built well without reference to politics. His embrace of naval politics long after his retirement from active duty was not the aberration it might seem to be. A careful examination of Togo's record reveals a number of incidents in which he exhibited a strong national spirit as well as dislike of foreigners. He was, after all, a samurai before he was a sailor. His real error of judgment was his failure to recognize the limitations of Japan, and that came about largely because of the generational differences between Togo and the other two figures treated here.

General Yamashita was a purely military man, a brilliant soldier, but totally incapable of coping with the social problems of the military of his time. He could only lament the irresponsibility of his military peers in letting the Japanese army run away with itself.

Of these three military leaders of Japan, Admiral Yamamoto was the most prescient. He understood the world around him better than the other two, or, in fact, better than most of his contemporaries. He saw no profit in the Manchurian takeover and even less in the militarization of Japan in an attempt to conquer China. Above all, Yamamoto understood the place of Japan in its world. He shared the ideal of Japanese leadership of Asia but did not believe the path should lead to war with the West, and that such a war would be disastrous to Japan. He turned out to be precisely correct.

These three leaders represent the best of Japan of their times, the inability of Yamamoto and Yamashita to change the course of history notwithstanding. They did their best, working with the tools at their disposal. In their efforts they left a legacy of which Japan can be proud.

Bibliography

Beasley, W. G. *The Rise of Modern Japan*. London: Weidenfeld and Nicolson, 1990.

Blond, Georges. *Admiral Togo*. New York.: Macmillan, 1960.

Boei Sen Shi Shitsu Ara. *Sen Shi Sosho*. 101 vols. Tokyo: Asagumo Shinbun Sha.

Dull, Paul S. *Battle History of the Imperial Japanese Navy*. Annapolis: Naval Institute Press, 1978.

Gubbins, W. *The Making of Modern Japan*. Freeport, N.Y.: Books for Libraries Press, 1971.

Harrington, Clifford. *The Silent Samurai of the Sea*. Tokyo Information Publishing Ltd., u.d.

Hoyt, Edwin P. *Pacific Destiny*. New York: W.W. Norton, 1981.

—*The New Militarists*. New York: Donald A. Fine, 1985.

—*Yamamoto*. New York: McGraw Hill, 1990.

Jane, Fred. *The Imperial Japanese Navy*. London: Conway Maritime Press, 1904.

Kennedy, M. D. *Some Aspects of Japan and Her Defense Forces*, London: Kean Paul Trench Trubner, 1928.

Lael, Richard I. *The Yamashita Precedent*. Wilmington, Del.: Scholarly Resources Inc., 1982.

Morley, James William. *Japan Erupts*. New York: Columbia University Press, 1984.

U.S. Naval Institute. *The Japanese Navy In World War II*, Annapolis: Naval Institute Press, 1967.

Pelz, S. E. *The Race to Pearl Harbor*, Cambridge: Harvard University Press, 1974.

Potter, John Dean. *The Life and Death of a Japanese General (Tomoyuki Yamashita)*. New York: New American Library, 1962.

—*Admiral of the Pacific*. London: Heinemann, 1965.

Reel, A. Frank. *The Case of General Yamashita*. New York: Octagon Books, 1971.

Swinson, Arthur. *Four Samurai*. London: Hutchinson, 1968.

Taylor, Lawrence, *A Trial of Generals*. South Bend, Ind.: Icarus Press, 1981.

Watts, A. P., and Brian G. Gordon. *Imperial Japanese Navy*. London: MacDonald, 1971.

Index